Contents

GRILLED CHEESE SANDWICH

Servings: 2 | Prep: 5m | Cooks: 15m | Total: 20m

NUTRITION FACTS

Calories: 400 | Carbohydrates: 25.7g | Fat: 28.3g | Protein: 11.1g | Cholesterol: 76mg

INGREDIENTS

- 4 slices white bread
- 3 tablespoons butter, divided
- 2 slices Cheddar cheese

DIRECTIONS

1. Preheat skillet over medium heat. Generously butter one side of a slice of bread. Place bread butter-side-down onto skillet bottom and add 1 slice of cheese. Butter a second slice of bread on one side and place butter-side-up on top of sandwich. Grill until lightly browned and flip over; continue grilling until cheese is melted. Repeat with remaining 2 slices of bread, butter and slice of cheese.

BEST TUNA MELT (NEW JERSEY DINER STYLE)

Servings: 4 | Prep: 10m | Cooks: 5m | Total: 15m

NUTRITION FACTS

Calories: 484 | Carbohydrates: 22.1g | Fat: 28.4g | Protein: 34.8g | Cholesterol: 76mg

INGREDIENTS

- 2 (5 ounce) cans tuna, drained
- 1 pinch salt
- 1/4 cup mayonnaise
- 1 pinch freshly ground black pepper
- 1/4 cup finely chopped celery
- 4 slices seedless rye bread
- 1 1/2 tablespoons finely chopped onion
- 8 slices ripe tomato
- 1 tablespoon chopped parsley
- 8 slices Swiss cheese
- 3/4 teaspoon red wine vinegar
- paprika, for garnish

DIRECTIONS

1. Preheat the oven broiler.
2. In a bowl, mix the tuna, mayonnaise, celery, onion, parsley, and vinegar. Season with salt and pepper.
3. Place the rye bread slices on a baking sheet, and broil 1 minute in the preheated oven, until lightly toasted. Remove from heat, and spread with the tuna salad. Place 1 cheese slice over the tuna salad on each piece of bread, layer with a tomato slice, and top with remaining cheese slices.
4. Return layered bread to the preheated oven, and broil 3 to 5 minutes, until cheese is melted.

MAKE AHEAD LUNCH WRAPS
Servings: 16 | Prep: 30m | Cooks: 35m | Total: 1h5m

NUTRITION FACTS

Calories: 557 | Carbohydrates: 80.8g | Fat: 16g | Protein: 22.9g | Cholesterol: 30mg

INGREDIENTS

- 2 cups uncooked brown rice
- 1 (10 ounce) can whole kernel corn
- 4 cups water
- 1 (10 ounce) can diced tomatoes and green chiles
- 4 (15 ounce) cans black beans
- 16 (10 inch) flour tortillas
- 2 (15.5 ounce) cans pinto beans
- 1 pound shredded pepperjack cheese

DIRECTIONS

1. Combine rice and water in a saucepan, and bring to a boil. Reduce heat to low, cover, and simmer for 35 to 40 minutes, or until tender. Remove from heat, and cool.
2. Place black beans and pinto beans into a colander or strainer, and rinse. Add corn and diced tomatoes with green chilies, and toss to mix. Transfer to a large bowl, and mix in rice and cheese.
3. Divide the mixture evenly among the tortillas, and roll up. Wrap individually in plastic wrap, place into a large freezer bag, and freeze. Reheat as needed in the microwave for lunch or snacks.

PEPPERONI BREAD
Servings: 10 | Prep: 15m | Cooks: 40m | Total: 2h55m | Additional: 2h

NUTRITION FACTS

Calories: 233 | Carbohydrates: 22.5g | Fat: 10.1g | Protein: 11.4g | Cholesterol: 38mg

INGREDIENTS

- 1 (1 pound) loaf frozen bread dough, thawed
- 1 cup shredded mozzarella cheese
- 1 egg, beaten
- 1/4 cup grated Parmesan cheese
- 4 ounces sliced pepperoni sausage
- 1 1/2 teaspoons Italian seasoning

DIRECTIONS

1. Preheat oven to 375 degrees F (190 degrees C). Lightly grease a baking sheet.
2. Roll frozen bread dough out into a rectangle. Brush dough with beaten egg. Arrange pepperoni, mozzarella cheese and parmesan cheese over the dough. Sprinkle on the Italian seasoning. Roll up dough like a jelly roll and pinch seam to seal; place, seam side down, on prepared baking sheet.
3. Bake in preheated oven for 40 minutes, or until golden.

REUBEN SANDWICH
Servings: 4 | Prep: 15m | Cooks: 10m | Total: 25m

NUTRITION FACTS

Calories: 657 | Carbohydrates: 43.5g | Fat: 40.3g | Protein: 32.1g | Cholesterol: 115mg

INGREDIENTS

- 2 tablespoons butter
- 8 slices Swiss cheese
- 8 slices rye bread
- 1 cup sauerkraut, drained
- 8 slices deli sliced corned beef
- 1/2 cup Thousand Island dressing

DIRECTIONS

1. Lightly butter one side of bread slices. Spread non-buttered sides with Thousand Island dressing. On 4 bread slices, layer 1 slice Swiss cheese, 2 slices corned beef, 1/4 cup sauerkraut and second slice of Swiss cheese. Top with remaining bread slices, buttered sides out.
2. Grill sandwiches until both sides are golden brown, about 5 minutes per side. Serve hot.
3. Preheat a large skillet or griddle on medium heat.

SLOPPY JOES
Servings: 6 | Prep: 15m | Cooks: 40m | Total: 55m

NUTRITION FACTS

Calories: 271 | Carbohydrates: 14.4g | Fat: 12.6g | Protein: 24.6g | Cholesterol: 84mg

INGREDIENTS

- 1 1/2 pounds extra lean ground beef
- 1 teaspoon Dijon mustard
- 1/2 onion, diced
- 1 dash Worcestershire sauce
- 2 cloves garlic, minced
- 1 1/2 teaspoons salt, or to taste
- 1 green bell pepper, diced
- 1/2 teaspoon ground black pepper
- 1 cup water
- 1 cup water
- 3/4 cup ketchup
- 1 pinch cayenne pepper, or to taste
- 2 tablespoons brown sugar

DIRECTIONS

1. Combine the ground beef and onion in a cold skillet, place the skillet onto a stove burner, and turn the heat to medium; cook and stir until the beef is crumbly and browned. Stir the garlic and bell pepper into the beef mixture; continue cooking and stirring until the vegetables are tender, 2 to 3 more minutes. Add 1 cup of water. Mix in ketchup, brown sugar, Dijon mustard, Worcestershire, salt, and pepper. Pour in 1 more cup of water. Bring to a simmer. Reduce heat to low and cook until the mixture becomes very thick, 30 to 45 minutes. Adjust salt and pepper as needed. Season with cayenne.

HOMEMADE SLOPPY JOES
Servings: 6 | Prep: 15m | Cooks: 55m | Total: 1h10m

NUTRITION FACTS

Calories: 251 | Carbohydrates: 14.4g | Fat: 11.9g | Protein: 21.5g | Cholesterol: 69mg

INGREDIENTS

- 1 1/2 pounds extra lean ground beef
- 2 tablespoons brown sugar
- 1/2 onion, diced
- 1 teaspoon Dijon mustard
- 2 cloves garlic, minced
- 1 1/2 teaspoons salt, or to taste
- 1 green pepper, diced

- 1/2 teaspoon ground black pepper
- 1 cup water
- 1 cup water
- 3/4 cup ketchup
- cayenne pepper to taste (optional)
- 1 dash Worcestershire sauce

DIRECTIONS

1. Place ground beef and onion in a large skillet. Turn heat to medium and cook and stir the mixture constantly until the beef is browned and forms small crumbles, about 10 minutes.
2. Stir in garlic and green bell pepper; cook and stir until softened, 2 to 3 minutes. Add 1 cup water and stir, scraping the pan to dissolve any brown flavor bits from the bottom of the skillet.
3. Mix in ketchup, Worcestershire sauce, brown sugar, Dijon mustard, salt, and black pepper. Add 1 more cup water and return mixture to a simmer. Reduce heat to low and simmer, stirring occasionally, until the liquid has evaporated and the mixture is thick, about 40 minutes.
4. Season with salt , black pepper, and cayenne pepper to taste.

CHICKEN SOUVLAKI GYRO STYLE

Servings: 4 | Prep: 30m | Cooks: 20m | Total: 1h50m | Additional: 1h

NUTRITION FACTS

Calories: | Carbohydrates: g | Fat: g | Protein: g | Cholesterol: mg

INGREDIENTS

- 3/4 cup balsamic vinaigrette salad dressing
- 1 clove garlic, minced
- 3 tablespoons lemon juice
- 1 tablespoon chopped fresh dill
- 1 tablespoon dried oregano
- 1/2 teaspoon Greek seasoning
- 1/2 teaspoon freshly ground black pepper
- 1 pinch kosher salt to taste
- 4 skinless, boneless chicken breast halves
- 1 pinch freshly ground black pepper to taste
- 1/2 cup seeded, shredded cucumber
- 4 large pita bread rounds
- 1 teaspoon kosher salt
- 1 heart of romaine lettuce, cut into 1/4 inch slices
- 1 cup plain yogurt
- 1 red onion, thinly sliced

- 1/4 cup sour cream
- 1 tomato, halved and sliced
- 1 tablespoon lemon juice
- 1/2 cup kalamata olives
- 1/2 tablespoon rice vinegar
- 1/2 cup pepperoncini
- 1 teaspoon olive oil
- 1 cup crumbled feta cheese

DIRECTIONS

1. Place ground beef and onion in a large skillet. Turn heat to medium and cook and stir the mixture constantly until the beef is browned and forms small crumbles, about 10 minutes.
2. Stir in garlic and green bell pepper; cook and stir until softened, 2 to 3 minutes. Add 1 cup water and stir, scraping the pan to dissolve any brown flavor bits from the bottom of the skillet.
3. Mix in ketchup, Worcestershire sauce, brown sugar, Dijon mustard, salt, and black pepper. Add 1 more cup water and return mixture to a simmer. Reduce heat to low and simmer, stirring occasionally, until the liquid has evaporated and the mixture is thick, about 40 minutes.
4. Season with salt , black pepper, and cayenne pepper to taste.

FABULOUS ZUCCHINI GRINDERS

Servings: 4 | Prep: 20m | Cooks: m | Total: 50m

NUTRITION FACTS

Calories: 339 | Carbohydrates: 37.3g | Fat: 15.1g | Protein: 16.9g | Cholesterol: 35mg

INGREDIENTS

- 1 tablespoon olive oil
- salt and pepper to taste
- 2 cloves garlic, peeled and coarsely chopped
- 1 tablespoon butter
- 1 pinch crushed red pepper flakes
- 2 medium zucchini, cubed
- 1 tablespoon chopped fresh basil
- 1 pinch red pepper flakes
- 1 teaspoon red wine vinegar
- salt and pepper to taste
- 1 teaspoon white sugar
- 1 1/2 cups shredded mozzarella cheese
- 1 (14.5 ounce) can diced tomatoes
- 4 (6 inch) French or Italian sandwich rolls, split

DIRECTIONS

1. To make marinara sauce, heat olive oil in a saucepan over medium heat (see Cook's Note). Add garlic, basil and red pepper flakes; cook and stir for a minute or two until fragrant. Stir in sugar, vinegar, salt, and pepper. Pour in tomatoes with their juices and simmer over low heat for 15 minutes. Remove from heat and puree until smooth in food processor or blender.
2. Preheat the oven to 350 degrees F (175 degrees C).
3. Melt butter in a skillet over medium heat. Cook the zucchini in butter until browned and slightly tender. Season with red pepper flakes, salt, and pepper.
4. Spoon a generous amount of the zucchini mixture into each sandwich roll. Cover zucchini with about 1/4 cup marinara sauce per roll. Top with a handful of shredded mozzarella. Close the rolls, and wrap individually in aluminum foil.
5. Bake for 15 minutes in the preheated oven, until bread is heated through, rolls are soft, and cheese is melted.

MAMA'S BEST BROILED TOMATO SANDWICH
Servings: 2 | Prep: 10m | Cooks: 5m | Total: 15m

NUTRITION FACTS

Calories: 509 | Carbohydrates: 43.2g | Fat: 34.8g | Protein: 9.6g | Cholesterol: 14mg

INGREDIENTS

- 2 tablespoons olive oil
- 1/4 teaspoon dried oregano
- 2 tablespoons balsamic vinegar
- 1/4 teaspoon black pepper
- 4 ripe tomatoes, sliced
- 3 tablespoons grated Parmesan cheese, divided
- 3 tablespoons mayonnaise
- 4 slices bread, lightly toasted
- 1/2 teaspoon dried parsley

DIRECTIONS

1. Preheat oven to broil.
2. In a shallow bowl, whisk together the olive oil and vinegar. Marinate the tomatoes in the mixture, stirring occasionally.
3. Meanwhile, in a small bowl, combine mayonnaise, parsley, oregano, black pepper and 4 teaspoons Parmesan cheese. Spread mixture on each slice of toasted bread. Place marinated tomatoes on 2 slices and sprinkle with remaining Parmesan cheese.
4. Place on a baking sheet and broil for 5 minutes, or until cheese turns golden brown. Serve immediately, open faced or closed.

CUBAN MIDNIGHT SANDWICH

Servings: 4 | Prep: 20m | Cooks: 5m | Total: 25m

NUTRITION FACTS

Calories: 1096 | Carbohydrates: 44.1g | Fat: 84.7g | Protein: 43.3g | Cholesterol: 127mg

INGREDIENTS

- 1 cup mayonnaise
- 1/2 pound thinly sliced cooked ham
- 5 tablespoons Italian dressing
- 1/2 pound thinly sliced Swiss cheese
- 4 hoagie rolls, split lengthwise
- 1 cup dill pickle slices
- 4 tablespoons prepared mustard
- 1/2 cup olive oil
- 1/2 pound thinly sliced deli turkey meat

DIRECTIONS

1. In a small bowl, mix together mayonnaise and Italian dressing. Spread mixture on hoagie rolls. Spread each roll with mustard. On each roll, arrange layers of turkey, ham, and cheese. Top each with dill pickle slices. Close sandwiches, and brush tops and bottoms with olive oil.
2. Heat a non-stick skillet over medium high heat. Place sandwiches in skillet. Cook sandwiches for 2 minutes, pressing down with a plate covered with aluminum foil. Flip, and cook for 2 more minutes, or until cheese is melted. Remove from heat, place on plates, and cut in half diagonally.

AWESOME GRILLED CHEESE SANDWICHES

Servings: 9 | Prep: 10m | Cooks: 15m | Total: 25m

NUTRITION FACTS

Calories: 293 | Carbohydrates: 25.7g | Fat: 16.2g | Protein: 10.9g | Cholesterol: 43mg

INGREDIENTS

- 18 slices bread
- 9 slices Cheddar cheese
- 4 tablespoons butter

DIRECTIONS

1. Preheat oven to 450 degrees F (230 degrees C).

2. Butter one side of 9 slices of bread, and place butter-side down on a baking sheet. Arrange cheese on each slice of bread. Spread butter on 9 remaining slices of bread, and place them buttered-side up on top of the cheese.
3. Bake in preheated oven for 6 to 8 minutes. Flip the sandwiches, and bake an additional 6 to 8 minutes, or until golden brown.

TURKEY SLOPPY JOES
Servings: 6 | Prep: 10m | Cooks: 30m | Total: 40m

NUTRITION FACTS

Calories: 394 | Carbohydrates: 36.8g | Fat: 16.5g | Protein: 25.9g | Cholesterol: 90mg

INGREDIENTS

- 2 tablespoons butter
- 1/2 teaspoon cayenne pepper, or to taste
- 1 onion, diced
- 1/2 teaspoon Worcestershire sauce
- salt and ground black pepper to taste
- 1/2 teaspoon unsweetened cocoa powder
- 1 1/4 pounds ground turkey
- 1 cup water, or as needed
- 1/2 cup cold water
- 6 hamburger buns, split
- 3/4 cup ketchup
- 1/3 cup chopped green onions
- 1 1/2 tablespoons brown sugar
- 1/2 cup shredded white Cheddar cheese

DIRECTIONS

1. Melt butter in a heavy skillet over medium heat. Add onion; cook and stir until onion starts to brown, about 5 minutes. Season with salt and black.
2. Mix ground turkey and 1/2 cup cold water into onions. Cook and stir, breaking up the meat, until it begins to brown, about 2 minutes. Add ketchup, brown sugar, cayenne pepper, salt, and black pepper. Cook and stir until liquid is reduced, about 5 minutes. Stir in Worcestershire sauce and cocoa powder. Cook, stirring frequently and adding up to 1 cup water if needed, until meat is cooked through and liquid is reduced and thick, 20 to 30 minutes.
3. Preheat the oven's broiler and set the oven rack about 6 inches from the heat source. Toast hamburger buns until golden, 2 to 3 minutes.
4. Remove turkey mixture from the heat and mix in green onions and Cheddar cheese. Serve on toasted hamburger buns.

SLOW COOKER BBQ CHICKEN
Servings: 8 | Prep: 5m | Cooks: 6h30m | Total: 6h35m

NUTRITION FACTS

Calories: 588.5 | Carbohydrates: 90g | Fat: 0g | Protein: 34.2g | Cholesterol: 58.5mg

INGREDIENTS

- 4 large skinless, boneless chicken breast halves
- 2 tablespoons Worcestershire sauce
- 1 cup ketchup
- 1/2 teaspoon chili powder
- 2 tablespoons mustard
- 1/8 teaspoon cayenne pepper
- 2 teaspoons lemon juice
- 2 dashes hot pepper sauce, or to taste
- 1/4 teaspoon garlic powder
- 8 eaches sandwich rolls, split
- 1/2 cup maple syrup

DIRECTIONS

1. Place the chicken breasts into the bottom of a slow cooker. In a bowl, stir together the ketchup, mustard, lemon juice, garlic powder, maple syrup, Worcestershire sauce, chili powder, cayenne pepper, and hot sauce until the mixture is well blended.
2. Pour the sauce over the chicken, set the cooker to Low, and cook for 6 hours. Shred the chicken with two forks, and cook for 30 more minutes. Serve the chicken and sauce spooned into the sandwich rolls.

MINI HAM AND CHEESE ROLLS
Servings: 24 | Prep: 15m | Cooks: 20m | Total: 35m

NUTRITION FACTS

Calories: 145 | Carbohydrates: 10.2g | Fat: 9g | Protein: 5.7g | Cholesterol: 18mg

INGREDIENTS

- 2 tablespoons dried minced onion
- 24 dinner rolls
- 1 tablespoon prepared mustard
- 1/2 pound chopped ham
- 2 tablespoons poppy seeds

- 1/2 pound thinly sliced Swiss cheese
- 1/2 cup margarine, melted

DIRECTIONS

1. Preheat oven to 325 degrees F (165 degrees C).
2. In a small mixing bowl, combine onion flakes, mustard, poppy seeds and margarine.
3. Split each dinner roll. Make a sandwich of the ham and cheese and the dinner rolls. Arrange the sandwiches on a baking sheet. Drizzle the poppy seed mixture over the sandwiches.
4. Bake for 20 minutes, or until cheese has melted. Serve these sandwiches warm.

CUCUMBER SANDWICH

Servings: 1 | Prep: 10m | Cooks: 0m | Total: 10m

NUTRITION FACTS

Calories: 496 | Carbohydrates: 46.3g | Fat: 32.5g | Protein: 11.4g | Cholesterol: 32mg

INGREDIENTS

- 2 thick slices whole wheat bread
- 1 teaspoon red wine vinegar
- 2 tablespoons cream cheese, softened
- 1 tomato, sliced
- 6 slices cucumber
- 1 leaf lettuce
- 2 tablespoons alfalfa sprouts
- 1 ounce pepperoncini, sliced
- 1 teaspoon olive oil
- 1/2 avocado, mashed

DIRECTIONS

1. Spread each slice of bread with 1 tablespoon cream cheese. On one slice of bread, arrange cucumber slices in a single layer. Cover with sprouts, then sprinkle with oil and vinegar. Layer tomato slices, lettuce, and pepperoncini. Spread other slice of bread with mashed avocado. Close sandwich and serve immediately.

GRILLED PEANUT BUTTER AND JELLY SANDWICH

Servings: 1 | Prep: 5m | Cooks: 8m | Total: 13m

NUTRITION FACTS

Calories: 273 | Carbohydrates: 35.5g | Fat: 12.5g | Protein: 5.3g | Cholesterol: 22mg

INGREDIENTS

- 2 teaspoons butter
- 1 teaspoon peanut butter
- 2 slices white bread
- 2 teaspoons any flavor fruit

DIRECTIONS

1. Heat griddle or skillet to 350 degrees F (175 degrees C).
2. Spread butter on one side of each slice of bread. Spread peanut butter on unbuttered side of one slice of bread, and jelly on the other. Place one slice, buttered side down on the griddle. Top with other slice, so that peanut butter and jelly are in the middle. Cook for 4 minutes on each side, or until golden brown, and heated through.

DASH'S DONAIR

Servings: 4 | Prep: 30m | Cooks: 1h15m | Total: 1h45m

NUTRITION FACTS

Calories: 489 | Carbohydrates: 49.5g | Fat: 20.9g | Protein: 26g | Cholesterol: 98mg

INGREDIENTS

- 1 teaspoon salt
- 1/4 teaspoon cayenne pepper
- 1 teaspoon ground oregano
- 1 pound ground beef
- 1 teaspoon all-purpose flour
- 1 (12 fluid ounce) can evaporated milk
- 1/2 teaspoon ground black pepper
- 3/4 cup white sugar
- 1/2 teaspoon Italian seasoning
- 2 teaspoons garlic powder
- 1/2 teaspoon garlic powder
- 4 teaspoons white vinegar, or as needed
- 1/2 teaspoon onion powder

DIRECTIONS

1. Preheat the oven to 350 degrees F (175 degrees C). In a cup or small bowl, mix together the salt, oregano, flour, black pepper, Italian seasoning, garlic powder, onion powder, and cayenne pepper.
2. Place the ground beef in a large bowl, and use your hands to blend in the spice mixture. If you want the smooth texture of meat that you see in a real donair shop, you must do this in a steel mixing bowl

and on a sturdy surface. Pick up the meat, and throw it down with force about 20 times, kneading it after each throw. This also helps the meat hold together better when you slice it.

3. rm the meat into a loaf, and place it on a broiler pan. If you do not have one, a baking sheet will do.

4. Bake for 1 hour and 15 minutes in the preheated oven, turning the loaf over about half way through. This will ensure even cooking. Serve, or allow the meat to chill before slicing and reheating.

5. To make the donair sauce, mix together the evaporated milk, sugar and garlic powder in a medium bowl. Gradually whisk in the white vinegar, adding 1 teaspoon at a time, until thickened to your desired consistency.

EASY HAM AND CHEESE APPETIZER SANDWICHES
Servings: 12 | Prep: 15m | Cooks: 12m | Total: 30m | Additional: 3m

NUTRITION FACTS

Calories: 416 | Carbohydrates: 31.4g | Fat: 27.7g | Protein: 12.11g | Cholesterol: 63mg

INGREDIENTS

- 1 cup butter, softened
- 2 tablespoons prepared Dijon-style mustard
- 3 tablespoons poppy seeds
- 2 (12 ounce) packages white party rolls
- 1 onion, grated
- 1/2 pound chopped cooked ham
- 1 tablespoon Worcestershire sauce
- 5 ounces shredded Swiss cheese

DIRECTIONS

1. Preheat oven to 350 degrees F (175 degrees C).
2. In a medium bowl, mix together butter, poppy seeds, onion, Worcestershire sauce and prepared Dijon-style mustard.
3. Slice rolls in half horizontally and set aside tops. Spread bottoms with the butter mixture. Top with ham and Swiss cheese. Replace tops.
4. Arrange rolls in a single layer in a medium baking dish. Bake in the preheated oven 10 to 12 minutes, until rolls are lightly browned and cheese is melted.

PHILLY STEAK SANDWICH
Servings: 4 | Prep: 15m | Cooks: 25m | Total: 40m

NUTRITION FACTS

Calories: 641 | Carbohydrates: 39.5g | Fat: 38.4g | Protein: 35.3g | Cholesterol: 96mg

INGREDIENTS

- 1 pound beef sirloin, cut into thin 2 inch strips
- 1/2 teaspoon dried marjoram
- 1/2 teaspoon salt
- 1/2 teaspoon dried basil
- 1/2 teaspoon black pepper
- 3 tablespoons vegetable oil
- 1/2 teaspoon paprika
- 1 onion, sliced
- ½ teaspoon chili powder
- 1 green bell pepper, julienned
- 1/2 teaspoon onion powder
- 3 ounces Swiss cheese, thinly sliced
- 1/2 teaspoon garlic powder
- 4 hoagie rolls, split lengthwise
- 1/2 teaspoon dried thyme

DIRECTIONS

1. Place the beef in a large bowl. In a small bowl, mix together salt, pepper, paprika, chili powder, onion powder, garlic powder, thyme, marjoram and basil. Sprinkle over beef.
2. Heat half of the oil in a skillet over medium-high heat. Saute beef to desired doneness, and remove from pan. Heat the remaining oil in the skillet, and saute the onion and green pepper.
3. Preheat oven on broiler setting.
4. Divide the meat between the bottoms of 4 rolls, layer with onion and green pepper, then top with sliced cheese. Place on cookie sheet, and broil until cheese is melted. Cover with tops of rolls, and serve.

TRADITIONAL GYRO MEAT

Servings: 10 | Prep: 15m | Cooks: 45m | Total: 2h | Additional: 1h

NUTRITION FACTS

Calories: 179 | Carbohydrates: 1.9g | Fat: 11.7g | Protein: 15.7g | Cholesterol: 59mg

INGREDIENTS

- 1/2 onion, cut into chunks
- 1 teaspoon dried marjoram
- 1 pound ground lamb
- 1 teaspoon ground dried rosemary
- 1 pound ground beef

- 1 teaspoon ground dried thyme
- 1 tablespoon minced garlic
- 1 teaspoon ground black pepper
- 1 teaspoon dried oregano
- 1/4 teaspoon sea salt
- 1 teaspoon ground cumin

DIRECTIONS

1. Place the onion in a food processor, and process until finely chopped. Scoop the onions onto the center of a towel, gather up the ends of the towel, and squeeze out the liquid from the onions. Place the onions into a mixing bowl along with the lamb and beef. Season with the garlic, oregano, cumin, marjoram, rosemary, thyme, black pepper, and salt. Mix well with your hands until well combined. Cover, and refrigerate 1 to 2 hours to allow the flavors to blend.
2. Preheat oven to 325 degrees F (165 degrees C).
3. Place the meat mixture into the food processor, and pulse for about a minute until finely chopped and the mixture feels tacky. Pack the meat mixture into a 7x4 inch loaf pan, making sure there are no air pockets. Line a roasting pan with a damp kitchen towel. Place the loaf pan on the towel, inside the roasting pan, and place into the preheated oven. Fill the roasting pan with boiling water to reach halfway up the sides of the loaf pan.
4. Bake until the gyro meat is no longer pink in the center, and the internal temperature registers 165 degrees F (75 degrees C) on a meat thermometer, 45 minutes to 1 hour. Pour off any accumulated fat, and allow to cool slightly before slicing thinly and serving.

ITALIAN GRILLED CHEESE SANDWICHES
Servings: 6 | Prep: 8m | Cooks: 7m | Total: 15m

NUTRITION FACTS

Calories: 394 | Carbohydrates: 42g | Fat: 18.3g | Protein: 15g | Cholesterol: 46mg

INGREDIENTS

- 1/4 cup unsalted butter
- 1 teaspoon dried oregano
- 1/8 teaspoon garlic powder (optional)
- 1 (8 ounce) package shredded mozzarella cheese
- 12 slices white bread
- 1 (24 ounce) jar vodka marinara sauce

DIRECTIONS

1. Preheat your oven's broiler.

2. Place 6 slices of bread onto a baking sheet. Spread a small handful of the mozzarella cheese over each slice. Top with the remaining 6 slices of bread. Mix together the butter and garlic powder, brush some over the tops of the sandwiches, or spread with the back of a tablespoon. Sprinkle with dried oregano.

3. Place baking sheet under the broiler for 2 to 3 minutes, until golden brown. Remove pan from oven, flip sandwiches, and brush the other sides with butter, and sprinkle with oregano. Return to the broiler, and cook until golden, about 2 minutes.

4. Cut sandwiches in half diagonally, and serve immediately with vodka sauce on the side for dipping.

SIMPLE SWEET AND SPICY CHICKEN WRAPS
Servings: 8 | Prep: 20m | Cooks: 15m | Total: 35m

NUTRITION FACTS

Calories: 488.1 | Carbohydrates: 44.7g | Fat: 0g | Protein: 26.6g | Cholesterol: 57.1mg

INGREDIENTS

- 1/2 cup mayonnaise
- 1 1/2 pounds skinless, boneless chicken breast halves - cut into thin strips
- 1/4 cup finely chopped seedless cucumber
- 1 cup thick and chunky salsa
- 1 tablespoon honey
- 1 tablespoon honey
- 1/2 teaspoon cayenne pepper
- 1/2 teaspoon cayenne pepper
- 1 pinch ground black pepper to taste
- 8 (10 inch) flour tortillas
- 2 tablespoons olive oil
- 1 (10 ounce) bag baby spinach

DIRECTIONS

1. Mix together the mayonnaise, cucumber, 1 tablespoon of honey, 1/2 teaspoon of cayenne pepper, and black pepper in a bowl until smooth. Cover and refrigerate until needed.

2. Heat the olive oil in a skillet on medium-high heat, and cook and stir the chicken breast strips until they are beginning to turn golden and are no longer pink in the middle, about 8 minutes. Stir in the salsa, 1 tablespoon of honey, and 1/2 teaspoon of cayenne pepper. Reduce the heat to medium-low and simmer, stirring occasionally, until the flavors have blended, about 5 minutes.

3. Stack the tortillas, 4 at a time, in a microwave oven and heat until warm and pliable, 20 to 30 seconds per batch.

4. Spread each tortilla with 1 tablespoon of the mayonnaise-cucumber mixture, top with a layer of baby spinach leaves, and arrange about 1/2 cup of chicken mixture on the spinach leaves.

5. Fold the bottom of each tortilla up about 2 inches, and start rolling the burrito from the right side. When the burrito is half-rolled, fold the top of the tortilla down, enclosing the filling, and continue rolling to make a tight, compact cylinder.

EMILY'S FAMOUS SLOPPY JOES
Servings: 8 | Prep: 10m | Cooks: 20m | Total: 30m

NUTRITION FACTS

Calories: 328 | Carbohydrates: 34.2g | Fat: 12.6g | Protein: 19.4g | Cholesterol: 52mg

INGREDIENTS

- 1 1/2 pounds ground beef
- 1 teaspoon ground cumin
- 1 onion, chopped
- 1 teaspoon distilled white vinegar
- 1 red bell pepper, chopped
- 3 tablespoons brown sugar
- 1 (6 ounce) can tomato paste
- 1 teaspoon dried oregano
- 1 cup water
- 1/2 teaspoon salt
- 3 cloves garlic, minced
- 1/2 teaspoon ground black pepper
- 1 tablespoon chili powder
- 8 hamburger buns, split
- 1 teaspoon paprika

DIRECTIONS

1. In a large skillet over medium-high heat, saute the ground beef for 5 minutes. Add the onion and red bell pepper; saute for 5 more minutes, or until onion is tender. Drain the fat.
2. Mix in tomato paste and water, stirring until paste is dissolved. Stir in garlic, chili powder, paprika, cumin, vinegar, brown sugar, oregano, salt and pepper. Continue to heat for 5 to 10 minutes, or until mixture is thick and stewy.

HOAGIE BAKE
Servings: 8 | Prep: 15m | Cooks: 35m | Total: 50m

NUTRITION FACTS

Calories: 619 | Carbohydrates: 24.9g | Fat: 44.8g | Protein: 30.9g | Cholesterol: 154mg

INGREDIENTS

- 2 (8 ounce) packages refrigerated crescent rolls
- 8 slices provolone cheese
- 1/4 pound salami, sliced
- 8 slices Swiss cheese
- 1/4 pound cooked ham, sliced
- 3 eggs, beaten
- 1/4 pound pepperoni sausage, sliced
- 2 tablespoons grated Parmesan cheese

DIRECTIONS

1. Preheat oven to 350 degrees F (175 degrees C). Coat a 9x13 inch baking dish with cooking spray.
2. Cover bottom of baking dish with 1 package crescent roll dough. Layer with salami, ham, and pepperoni. Cover meat with a layer of Provolone cheese and Swiss cheese. Spread 1/2 of the beaten eggs over the cheese. Top with second package of crescent rolls. Brush with remaining beaten eggs, and sprinkle with Parmesan cheese.
3. Bake, uncovered, in the preheated oven for 25 minutes. Cover with foil, and bake for another 10 minutes.

GRILLED PEANUT BUTTER AND BANANA SANDWICH
Servings: 1 | Prep: 2m | Cooks: 10m | Total: 12m

NUTRITION FACTS

Calories: 437 | Carbohydrates: 56.8g | Fat: 18.7g | Protein: 16.8g | Cholesterol: 0mg

INGREDIENTS

- cooking spray
- 2 slices whole wheat bread
- 2 tablespoons peanut butter
- 1 banana, sliced

DIRECTIONS

1. Heat a skillet or griddle over medium heat, and coat with cooking spray. Spread 1 tablespoon of peanut butter onto one side of each slice of bread. Place banana slices onto the peanut buttered side of one slice, top with the other slice and press together firmly. Fry the sandwich until golden brown on each side, about 2 minutes per side.

PESTO GRILLED CHEESE SANDWICH

Servings: 1 | Prep: 5m | Cooks: 10m | Total: 15m

NUTRITION FACTS

Calories: 503 | Carbohydrates: 24.2g | Fat: 36.5g | Protein: 20.4g | Cholesterol: 82mg

INGREDIENTS

- 2 slices Italian bread
- 1 slice provolone cheese
- 1 tablespoon softened butter, divided
- 2 slices tomato
- 1 tablespoon prepared pesto sauce, divided
- 1 slice American cheese

DIRECTIONS

1. Spread one side of a slice of bread with butter, and place it, buttered side down, into a nonstick skillet over medium heat.
2. Spread the top of the bread slice in the skillet with half the pesto sauce, and place a slice of provolone cheese, the tomato slices, and the slice of American cheese onto the pesto.
3. Spread remaining pesto sauce on one side of the second slice of bread, and place the bread slice, pesto side down, onto the sandwich. Butter the top side of the sandwich.
4. Gently fry the sandwich, flipping once, until both sides of the bread are golden brown and the cheese has melted, about 5 minutes per side.

GRANDMA'S SLOPPY JOES

Servings: 4 | Prep: 10m | Cooks: 45m | Total: 55m

NUTRITION FACTS

Calories: 429 | Carbohydrates: 47g | Fat: 16.2g | Protein: 24.9g | Cholesterol: 69mg

INGREDIENTS

- 1 pound ground beef
- 1 cup ketchup
- 1 cup chopped onion
- 2 tablespoons prepared mustard
- 1 cup chopped green bell pepper
- 1/2 teaspoon ground cloves
- 1 tablespoon brown sugar
- 1 teaspoon salt

- 1 tablespoon vinegar
- 4 hamburger buns, split

DIRECTIONS

1. In a large skillet over medium heat, combine the ground beef, onion, and green pepper. Cook until beef is browned, and drain off excess grease. Stir in the brown sugar, vinegar, ketchup and mustard, and season with cloves and salt. Simmer for 30 minutes on low. Serve on hamburger buns.

UNSLOPPY JOES

Servings: 8 | Prep: 15m | Cooks: 15m | Total: 30m

NUTRITION FACTS

Calories: 204 | Carbohydrates: 34.6g | Fat: 3.9g | Protein: 7.8g | Cholesterol: 0mg

INGREDIENTS

- 1 tablespoon olive oil
- 1 1/2 tablespoons chili powder
- 1/2 cup chopped onion
- 1 tablespoon tomato paste
- 1/2 cup chopped celery
- 1 tablespoon distilled white vinegar
- 1/2 cup chopped carrots
- 1 teaspoon ground black pepper
- 1/2 cup chopped green bell pepper
- 1 (15 ounce) can kidney beans, drained and rinsed
- 1 clove garlic, minced
- 8 kaiser rolls
- 1 (14.5 ounce) can diced tomatoes

DIRECTIONS

1. Heat olive oil in a large skillet over medium heat. Add onion, celery, carrot, green pepper, and garlic: saute until tender. Stir in tomatoes, chili powder, tomato paste, vinegar, and pepper. Cover, reduce heat, and simmer 10 minutes.
2. Stir in kidney beans, and cook an additional 5 minutes.
3. Cut a 1/4 inch slice off the top of each kaiser roll; set aside. Hollow out the center of each roll, leaving about 1/2 inch thick shells; reserve the inside of rolls for other uses.
4. Spoon bean mixture evenly into rolls and replace tops. Serve immediately.

MONTE CRISTO SANDWICH - THE REAL ONE
Servings: 8 | Prep: 10m | Cooks: 5m | Total: 15m

NUTRITION FACTS

Calories: 305 | Carbohydrates: 23.7g | Fat: 17.9g | Protein: 12.2g | Cholesterol: 50mg

INGREDIENTS

- 1 quart oil for frying, or as needed
- 8 slices white bread
- 2/3 cup water
- 4 slices Swiss cheese
- 1 egg
- 4 slices turkey
- 2/3 cup all-purpose flour
- 4 slices ham
- 1 3/4 teaspoons baking powder
- 1/8 teaspoon ground black pepper
- 1/2 teaspoon salt
- 1 tablespoon confectioners' sugar for dusting

DIRECTIONS

1. Heat 5 inches of oil in a deep-fryer to 365 degrees F (180 degrees C). While oil is heating, make the batter: In a medium bowl, whisk together the egg and water. Combine the flour, baking powder, salt and pepper; whisk into the egg mixture until smooth. Set aside in the refrigerator.
2. Assemble sandwiches by placing one slice of turkey on one slice of bread, a slice of ham on another, then sandwich them with the Swiss cheese in the middle. Cut sandwiches into quarters, and secure with toothpicks.
3. Dip each sandwich quarter in the batter so that all sides are coated. Deep fry in the hot oil until golden brown on all sides. Remove toothpicks and arrange on a serving tray. Dust with confectioners' sugar just before serving.

PORTOBELLO SANDWICHES
Servings: 4 | Prep: 8m | Cooks: 9m | Total: 20m

NUTRITION FACTS

Calories: 445 | Carbohydrates: 31.4g | Fat: 33.4g | Protein: 7.8g | Cholesterol: 5mg

INGREDIENTS

- 2 cloves garlic, minced
- 4 hamburger buns

- 6 tablespoons olive oil
- 1 tablespoon capers
- 1/2 teaspoon dried thyme
- 1/4 cup mayonnaise
- 2 tablespoons balsamic vinegar
- 1 tablespoon capers, drained
- salt and pepper to taste
- 1 large tomato, sliced
- 4 large portobello mushroom caps
- 4 leaves lettuce

DIRECTIONS

1. Turn on broiler, and adjust rack so it is as close to heat source as possible.
2. In a medium-size mixing bowl, mix together garlic, olive oil, thyme, vinegar, salt and pepper.
3. Put the mushroom caps, bottom side up, in a shallow baking pan. Brush the caps with 1/2 the dressing. Put the caps under the broiler, and cook for 5 minutes.
4. Turn the caps, and brush with the remaining dressing. Broil 4 minutes. Toast the buns lightly .
5. In a small bowl, mix capers and mayonnaise. Spread mayonnaise mixture on the buns, top with mushroom caps, tomato and lettuce.

GYROS BURGERS

Servings: 4 | Prep: 10m | Cooks: 15m | Total: 25m

NUTRITION FACTS

Calories: 338 | Carbohydrates: 5.7g | Fat: 25.4g | Protein: 20.3g | Cholesterol: 84mg

INGREDIENTS

- 1/2 pound lean ground beef
- 1/2 teaspoon ground allspice
- 1/2 pound lean ground lamb
- 1/2 teaspoon ground coriander
- 1/2 onion, grated
- 1/2 teaspoon salt
- 2 cloves garlic, pressed
- 1/2 teaspoon ground black pepper
- 1 slice bread, toasted and crumbled
- 1 dash ground cumin
- 1/2 teaspoon dried savory

DIRECTIONS

1. Preheat an outdoor grill for medium-high heat, and lightly oil grate.
2. In large bowl, combine ground beef, ground lamb, onion, garlic and bread crumbs. Season with savory, allspice, coriander, salt, pepper and cumin. Knead until mixture is stiff. Shape into 4 very thin patties (1/8 inch to 1/4 inch thick).
3. Cook patties for 5 to 7 minutes on each side, or until cooked through.

RUBY DRIVE SLOPPY JOES

Servings: 6 | Prep: 5m | Cooks: 30m | Total: 35m

NUTRITION FACTS

Calories: 382 | Carbohydrates: 46.2g | Fat: 15.2g | Protein: 17.4g | Cholesterol: 46mg

INGREDIENTS

- 1 pound ground beef
- 2 tablespoons white vinegar
- 1 1/2 cups ketchup
- 2 tablespoons Dijon mustard
- 1 cup chunky salsa
- 1 teaspoon hot sauce
- 2 tablespoons brown sugar
- 6 potato rolls
- 1 tablespoon Worcestershire sauce

DIRECTIONS

1. Heat a large skillet over medium-high heat and stir in the ground beef. Cook and stir until the beef is crumbly, evenly browned, and no longer pink. Drain and discard any excess grease.
2. Stir in ketchup, salsa, brown sugar, Worcestershire sauce, white vinegar, Dijon mustard, and hot sauce. Bring to a simmer and cook, stirring occasionally, over low heat 20 to 30 minutes. Serve on potato rolls.

SIMPLE STROMBOLI

Servings: 3 | Prep: 10m | Cooks: 30m | Total: 40m

NUTRITION FACTS

Calories: 1065 | Carbohydrates: 77.8g | Fat: 54.6g | Protein: 59g | Cholesterol: 162mg

INGREDIENTS

- 1/2 pound bulk pork sausage (optional)
- 4 slices American cheese

- 1 (1 pound) loaf frozen bread dough, thawed
- 1 cup shredded mozzarella cheese
- 4 slices hard salami
- salt and ground black pepper to taste
- 4 slices thinly sliced ham
- 1 egg white, lightly beaten

DIRECTIONS

1. Preheat oven to 425 degrees F (220 degrees C).
2. Heat a large skillet over medium-high heat; cook and stir sausage until crumbly, evenly browned, and no longer pink, about 10 minutes. Drain and discard any excess grease.
3. Pat out bread dough on an ungreased baking sheet, to 3/4-inch thickness. Lay salami, ham, and American cheese slices in center of dough. Sprinkle with mozzarella cheese, salt, pepper, and cooked sausage. Wrap dough to cover ingredients, pinching and sealing edges to prevent leakage; brush top with egg white.
4. Bake in preheated oven until dough is baked and lightly browned, 17 to 20 minutes.

PIGS IN A BLANKET

Servings: 6 | Prep: 10m | Cooks: 20m | Total: 30m

NUTRITION FACTS

Calories: 458 | Carbohydrates: 24.8g | Fat: 31.8g | Protein: 17.1g | Cholesterol: 57mg

INGREDIENTS

- 8 frankfurters
- 8 slices American processed cheese
- 1 (10 ounce) package refrigerated biscuit dough

DIRECTIONS

1. Preheat oven to 350 degrees F (175 degrees C).
2. Wrap cheese around each frankfurter then the biscuit around that. Put on cookie sheet with the overlap of biscuit faced down, so you don't have to use tooth picks.
3. Wrap cheese around each frankfurter then the biscuit around that. Put on cookie sheet with the overlap of biscuit faced down, so you don't have to use tooth picks.

SWEET AND SAVORY SLOW COOKER PULLED PORK

Servings: 10 | Prep: 20m | Cooks: 6h15m | Total: 15h5m | Additional: 8h30m

NUTRITION FACTS

Calories: 485 | Carbohydrates: 45.5g | Fat: 19.1g | Protein: 28.5g | Cholesterol: 81mg

INGREDIENTS

- 1 (4.5 pound) bone-in pork shoulder roast
- 1/4 teaspoon ground cinnamon
- 1 cup root beer
- 1/4 teaspoon ground ginger
- 2 1/2 tablespoons light brown sugar
- 1/4 teaspoon ground nutmeg
- 2 teaspoons kosher salt
- 1/3 cup balsamic vinegar
- 1/2 teaspoon ground black pepper
- 1 1/2 cups root beer
- 1 1/2 teaspoons ground paprika
- 1 1/2 fluid ounces whiskey
- 1/2 teaspoon dry mustard
- 1/4 cup brown sugar
- 1/2 teaspoon onion powder
- 1 tablespoon olive oil
- 1/4 teaspoon garlic salt
- 3/4 cup prepared barbecue sauce
- 1/4 teaspoon celery salt
- 10 hamburger buns, spli

DIRECTIONS

1. Place the pork shoulder roast into a large plastic bag, pour 1 cup of root beer over the meat, and squeeze out all the air from the bag. Seal the bag closed, and refrigerate 6 hours to overnight.
2. The next day, mix together the light brown sugar, kosher salt, black pepper, paprika, dry mustard, onion powder, garlic salt, celery salt, cinnamon, ginger, and nutmeg in a bowl.
3. Remove the meat from the marinade, and shake off the excess. Rub the meat all over with the spice mixture, wrap in plastic wrap, and refrigerate for 30 minutes to 2 hours.
4. Mix together the balsamic vinegar, 1 1/2 cups of root beer, whiskey, and brown sugar in a bowl, and stir until the sugar dissolves.
5. Heat the olive oil in a skillet over medium-high heat, and sear the meat on all sides until the meat develops a brown crust, about 3 minutes per side. Place the seared meat into a slow cooker. Pour the balsamic vinegar-root beer mixture over the meat, set the slow cooker to High, and cook for 6 to 8 hours.
6. Remove the roast from the slow cooker, and shred with 2 forks. Discard the bones and all but 1 cup of the liquid in the slow cooker. Return the shredded meat to the cooker, mix in the barbecue sauce, and let sit on Low until ready to serve. Serve piled on buns.

HAM AND CHEESE CRESCENT ROLL-UPS

Servings: 8 | Prep: 10m | Cooks: 15m | Total: 25m | Additional: 15m

NUTRITION FACTS

Calories: 164 | Carbohydrates: 11.2g | Fat: 10.2g | Protein: 5.6g | Cholesterol: 13mg

INGREDIENTS

- 1 (8 ounce) can Pillsbury Refrigerated Crescent Dinner Rolls
- 4 thin slices Cheddar cheese, cut into strips
- 8 thin slices cooked ham

DIRECTIONS

1. Heat oven to 350 degrees F. Separate dough into 8 triangles. Place 1 piece of ham on each triangle; place 2 strips of cheese down center of ham. Fold in edges of ham to match shape of dough triangle.
2. Roll up each crescent, ending at tip of triangle. Place with tips down on ungreased cookie sheet.
3. Bake 15 to 19 minutes or until golden brown. Immediately remove from cookie sheet. Serve warm.

DARRA'S FAMOUS TUNA WALDORF SALAD SANDWICH FILLING

Servings: 4 | Prep: 15m | Cooks: 5m | Total: 20m

NUTRITION FACTS

Calories: 695 | Carbohydrates: 42.4g | Fat: 48.9g | Protein: 23.1g | Cholesterol: 91mg

INGREDIENTS

- 1/2 cup mayonnaise
- 1/4 cup chopped walnuts
- 1 tablespoon prepared Dijon-style mustard
- 1/2 cup diced celery
- 1/4 teaspoon curry powder
- 1 teaspoon sweet pickle relish
- salt and pepper to taste
- 4 large croissants
- 1 (5 ounce) can tuna, drained
- 4 leaves lettuce
- 1 shallot, finely chopped
- 4 slices Swiss cheese
- 1 Granny Smith apple, cored and diced

DIRECTIONS

1. In a medium bowl, whisk together the mayonnaise, mustard, curry powder, salt and pepper. Add tuna, shallot, apple, walnuts, celery and pickle relish and toss until all ingredients are coated with dressing.
2. Lightly toast the croissants. Split in half, place a lettuce leaf on the bottom half of the croissant and fill with tuna salad. Top with a slice of Swiss cheese and the top half of the croissant. Serve with a dill pickle and potato chips. Bon appetite.

BACON JACK CHICKEN SANDWICH
Servings: 4 | Prep: 5m | Cooks: 20m | Total: 25m

NUTRITION FACTS

Calories: 482 | Carbohydrates: 27g | Fat: 0g | Protein: 41.7g | Cholesterol: 117.7mg

INGREDIENTS

- 8 slices bacon
- 4 leaves of lettuce
- 4 skinless, boneless chicken breast halves
- 4 slices tomato
- 2 teaspoons poultry seasoning
- 1/2 cup thinly sliced onions
- 4 slices pepperjack cheese
- 12 slices dill pickle
- 4 hamburger buns, split

DIRECTIONS

1. Preheat a grill for medium heat.
2. While the grill preheats, place the bacon in a large skillet over medium-high heat. Cook until browned on both sides. Remove from the pan, and drain on paper towels.
3. Rub the poultry seasoning onto the chicken pieces, and place them on the grill. Cook for about 6 minutes per side, or until no longer pink in the center. Top each piece of chicken with 2 slices of bacon and 1 slice of pepperjack cheese. Grill for 2 to 3 more minutes to melt the cheese.
4. Place each piece of chicken on a bun, and top with lettuce, tomato, onion and pickle slices before serving with your favorite condiments.

BUFFALO CHICKEN WRAPS
Servings: 4 | Prep: 20m | Cooks: 10m | Total: 30m

NUTRITION FACTS

Calories: 588.1 | Carbohydrates: 39.8g | Fat: 0g | Protein: 30.4g | Cholesterol: 82.8mg

INGREDIENTS

- 1 tablespoon vegetable oil
- 4 (10 inch) flour tortillas
- 1 tablespoon butter
- 2 cups shredded lettuce
- 1 pound skinless, boneless chicken breasts, cut into bite-size pieces
- 1 celery stalk, diced
- 1/4 cup hot sauce
- 1/2 cup blue cheese dressing

DIRECTIONS

1. Heat the vegetable oil and butter in a large skillet over medium-high heat. Place the chicken in the pan; cook and stir until the chicken is no longer pink in the center and the juices run clear, about 10 minutes. Remove the pan from the heat. Pour the hot sauce over the cooked chicken and toss to coat.
2. Lay out the flour tortillas and divide the chicken evenly among the tortillas. Top the chicken with lettuce, celery, and blue cheese dressing. Fold in the sides of the tortilla and roll the wrap burrito-style.

EGGPLANT SANDWICHES

Servings: 2 | Prep: 20m | Cooks: 10m | Total: 30m

NUTRITION FACTS

Calories: 802 | Carbohydrates: 91.3g | Fat: 39.5g | Protein: 23.8g | Cholesterol: 44mg

INGREDIENTS

- 1 small eggplant, halved and sliced
- 2 (6 inch) French sandwich rolls
- 1 tablespoon olive oil, or as needed
- 1 small tomato, sliced
- 1/4 cup mayonnaise
- 1/2 cup crumbled feta cheese
- 2 cloves garlic, minced
- 1/4 cup chopped fresh basil leaves

DIRECTIONS

1. Preheat your oven's broiler. Brush eggplant slices with olive oil, and place them on a baking sheet or broiling pan. Place the pan about 6 inches from the heat source. Cook under the broiler for 10 minutes, or until tender and toasted.
2. Split the French rolls lengthwise, and toast. In a cup or small bowl, stir together the mayonnaise and garlic. Spread this mixture on the toasted bread. Fill the rolls with eggplant slices, tomato, feta cheese and basil leaves.

TUNA MELTS
Servings: 8 | Prep: 15m | Cooks: 10m | Total: 25m

NUTRITION FACTS

Calories: 483 | Carbohydrates: 34.1g | Fat: 27.7g | Protein: 24.5g | Cholesterol: 41mg

INGREDIENTS

- 1 (1 pound) loaf French bread
- 2 cups mozzarella cheese, shredded
- 1 small sweet onion, peeled and diced
- 1 cup mayonnaise
- 1 (12 ounce) can tuna, drained

DIRECTIONS

1. Preheat oven to 350 degrees F (175 degrees C).
2. In a mixing bowl, combine sweet onion, drained tuna, mozzarella, and mayonnaise. Mix thoroughly.
3. Spread tuna mixture on slices of French bread to form a sandwich. Place sandwiches on a cookie sheet.
4. Bake in a preheated oven for 10 minutes.

GOURMET CHICKEN SANDWICH
Servings: 4 | Prep: 10m | Cooks: 15m | Total: 25m

NUTRITION FACTS

Calories: 522.5 | Carbohydrates: 58g | Fat: 0g | Protein: 34.6g | Cholesterol: 39.8mg

INGREDIENTS

- 4 skinless, boneless chicken breast halves - pounded to 1/4 inch thickness
- 2 tablespoons mayonnaise
- ground black pepper to taste
- 2 teaspoons prepared Dijon-style mustard
- 1 tablespoon olive oil

- 1 teaspoon chopped fresh rosemary
- 1 teaspoon minced garlic
- 8 slices garlic and rosemary focaccia bread

DIRECTIONS

1. Sprinkle pepper on one side of each chicken cutlet. Heat oil in a large skillet; brown garlic in oil, then add chicken, pepper-side-down. Saute chicken until cooked through and juices run clear, about 12 to 15 minutes.
2. In a small bowl combine the mayonnaise, mustard and rosemary. Mix together and spread mixture on 4 slices focaccia bread. Place 1 chicken cutlet on each of these slices, then top each with another bread slice.

JAN'S PRETZEL DOGS
Servings: 18 | Prep: 35m | Cooks: 35m | Total: 2h10m

NUTRITION FACTS

Calories: 299 | Carbohydrates: 27.2g | Fat: 15.8g | Protein: 9.7g | Cholesterol: 41mg

INGREDIENTS

- 1 (12 fluid ounce) can or bottle room temperature beer
- 1 large egg yolk
- 1 tablespoon white sugar
- 1 tablespoon water
- 2 teaspoons kosher salt
- 10 cups water
- 1 (.25 ounce) package active dry yeast
- 2/3 cup baking soda
- 4 1/2 cups bread flour
- 1/4 cup kosher salt, divided - or to taste
- 1/4 cup unsalted butter, melted
- 18 hot dogs

DIRECTIONS

1. Heat the beer in a saucepan over low heat until it reaches 110 degrees F (45 degrees C).
2. Combine the warm beer, sugar, and 2 teaspoons kosher salt in a bowl. Sprinkle the yeast on top, and let stand for 5 minutes until the yeast softens and begins to form a creamy foam.
3. Place the bread flour and butter in a bread machine. Add the yeast mixture, then select the dough cycle.
4. Preheat an oven to 450 degrees F (230 degrees C).
5. Line 2 baking sheets with parchment paper or grease with vegetable oil.

6. Beat the egg yolk in a small bowl with 1 tablespoon water; set aside.
7. Stir baking soda into 10 cups water in a large pot until dissolved, and bring to a boil.
8. Turn the dough out onto a lightly-oiled surface, and roll into a 10x20-inch rectangle.
9. Cut the dough into 18 1-inch wide strips, then wrap each strip tightly around a hot dog in a spiral, pinching the edges to seal, and leaving the ends open. About half an inch of hot dog should peek out of each end of the dough wrapper.
10. Drop 2 or 3 dough-wrapped hot dogs into the boiling water for 30 seconds.
11. Arrange the boiled hot dogs on the prepared baking sheets. Brush each pretzel dog with the egg yolk mixture, and sprinkle with the remaining 1/4 cup salt.
12. Bake in the preheated oven until golden brown, about 15 minutes.

B.L.A.T. WRAPS

Servings: 4 | Prep: 20m | Cooks: 20m | Total: 40m

NUTRITION FACTS

Calories: 643 | Carbohydrates: 43.9g | Fat: 46g | Protein: 14.1g | Cholesterol: 42mg

INGREDIENTS

- 8 slices bacon
- 1 avocado - peeled, pitted and diced
- 4 (10 inch) flour tortillas
- 1 tomato, chopped
- 4 tablespoons Ranch-style salad dressing
- 1 cup shredded lettuce

DIRECTIONS

1. Place bacon in a large, deep skillet. Cook over medium heat for 10 to 15 minutes, or until crisp. Drain, crumble, and set aside.
2. Warm tortillas in microwave oven for 30 to 45 seconds, or until soft. Spread 1 tablespoon Ranch dressing down the center of each tortilla. Layer crumbled bacon, avocado, tomato and lettuce over the dressing. Roll the tortilla around the other ingredients.

TANGY TURKEY AND SWISS SANDWICHES

Servings: 4 | Prep: 15m | Cooks: 10m | Total: 25m

NUTRITION FACTS

Calories: 856 | Carbohydrates: 42.6g | Fat: 58.9g | Protein: 41.9g | Cholesterol: 154mg

INGREDIENTS

- 3/4 cup chopped red onion

- 6 tablespoons butter, softened
- 1 tablespoon dried thyme
- 1 pound thinly sliced roast turkey
- 1/2 cup mayonnaise
- 8 slices tomato
- 1/4 cup coarse-grain brown mustard
- 8 slices Swiss cheese
- 8 slices country style French Bread

DIRECTIONS

1. In a small bowl, stir together the red onion, thyme, mayonnaise and mustard. Spread some of this mixture onto one side of each slice of bread. Spread butter onto the other side of the slices of bread.
2. Heat a large skillet over medium heat. Place 4 slices of the bread into the skillet with the butter side down. On each slice of bread, layer 1/4 of the sliced turkey, then 2 slices of tomato, and top with 2 slices of Swiss cheese. Place remaining slices of bread over the top with the butter side up. When the bottoms of the sandwiches are golden brown, flip over, and cook until golden on the other side.

BLT WRAPS

Servings: 4 | Prep: 15m | Cooks: 10m | Total: 25m

NUTRITION FACTS

Calories: 695 | Carbohydrates: 64.2g | Fat: 31.1g | Protein: 31.4g | Cholesterol: 71mg

INGREDIENTS

- 1 pound thick sliced bacon, cut into 1 inch pieces
- 1/2 head iceberg lettuce, shredded
- 4 (12 inch) flour tortillas
- 1 tomato, diced
- 1 cup shredded Cheddar cheese

DIRECTIONS

1. Place bacon in a large, deep skillet. Cook over medium-high heat until evenly brown. Drain, and set aside.
2. Place 1 tortilla on a microwave-safe plate. Sprinkle tortilla with 1/4 cup cheese. Cook in microwave 1 to 2 minutes, or until cheese is melted. Immediately top with 1/4 of the bacon, lettuce, and tomato. Fold sides of tortilla over, then roll up. Repeat with remaining ingredients. Cut each wrap in half before serving.

A PLUS FAIR CORN DOGS
Servings: 20 | Prep: 15m | Cooks: 4m | Total: 19m

NUTRITION FACTS

Calories: 248 | Carbohydrates: 13.6g | Fat: 18.4g | Protein: 6.9g | Cholesterol: 34mg

INGREDIENTS

- 1 quart oil for deep frying
- 2 tablespoons bacon drippings
- 1 cup all-purpose flour
- 1 egg, beaten
- 2/3 cup yellow cornmeal
- 1 1/4 cups buttermilk
- 1/4 cup white sugar
- 1/2 teaspoon baking soda
- 1 1/2 teaspoons baking powder
- 2 pounds hot dogs
- 1 teaspoon salt
- wooden sticks

DIRECTIONS

1. Heat oil in a deep fryer to 365 degrees F (185 degrees C).
2. In a large bowl, stir together the flour, cornmeal, sugar, baking powder and salt. Stir in melted bacon drippings. Make a well in the center, and pour in the egg, buttermilk, and baking soda. Mix until everything is smooth and well blended.
3. Pat the hot dogs dry with paper towels so that the batter will stick. Insert wooden sticks into the ends. Dip the hot dogs in the batter one at a time, shaking off the excess. Deep fry a few at a time in the hot oil until they are as brown as you like them. Drain on paper towels or serve on paper plates.

AMAZING SOUTHWEST CILANTRO LIME MANGO GRILLED CHICKEN SANDWICHES
Servings: 8 | Prep: 1h20m | Cooks: 20m | Total: 1h40m

NUTRITION FACTS

Calories: 554 | Carbohydrates: 54g | Fat: 0g | Protein: 29.4g | Cholesterol: 63.4mg

INGREDIENTS

- 1/4 cup finely chopped fresh cilantro
- 1/4 teaspoon ground black pepper

- 1 clove garlic, minced
- 1/4 teaspoon sea salt
- 1/4 jalapeno chile pepper, seeded and minced
- 1/8 teaspoon chipotle chile powder
- 2 tablespoons finely grated fresh lime zest
- 1 tablespoon fresh lime juice
- 1 1/2 teaspoons salt
- 1 sweet onion cut into 1/2-inch slices
- 1/2 teaspoon onion powder
- 1 red bell pepper, quartered
- 1/4 teaspoon ground black pepper
- 1 tablespoon olive oil
- 1/4 teaspoon chipotle chile powder
- 1/4 teaspoon salt
- 1 tablespoon olive oil
- 1/2 teaspoon minced garlic
- 1 pound chicken breast tenderloins or strips
- 1/2 cup mayonnaise
- 1 medium tomato, chopped
- 2 tablespoons fresh lime juice
- 1 small sweet onion, finely chopped
- 16 thick slices French bread
- 2 tablespoons finely chopped fresh cilantro
- 2 mangos - peeled, seeded, and sliced
- 1/2 jalapeno chile pepper, seeded and minced
- 8 slices Monterey Jack cheese
- 1 clove garlic, finely chopped

DIRECTIONS

1. For the marinade: Place 1/4 cup cilantro, 1 clove minced garlic, 1/4 jalapeno, lime zest, 1 1/2 teaspoons salt, onion powder, 1/4 teaspoon black pepper, 1/4 teaspoon chipotle chile powder, and 1 tablespoon olive oil in a small bowl and stir until well combined. Place the chicken breast tenderloins in a large resealable plastic bag. Pour the marinade into the bag with the chicken, seal, and shake the bag to coat. Refrigerate for 1 hour.
2. For the salsa: Combine the tomato, 1 small onion, 2 tablespoons cilantro, 1/2 jalapeno, 1 clove garlic, 1/4 teaspoon black pepper, sea salt, 1/8 teaspoon chipotle pepper, and 1 tablespoon lime juice in a bowl. Cover with plastic wrap and refrigerate.
3. To prepare the grilled vegetables, toss the onions and red peppers with 1 tablespoon olive oil, 1/4 teaspoon salt, and 1 clove garlic in a bowl; set aside.
4. For the lime mayonnaise: Whisk together the mayonnaise and 2 tablespoons of lime juice; cover with plastic wrap and refrigerate.

5. Preheat an outdoor grill for medium-high heat.
6. Grill the marinated chicken on the prepared grill until no longer pink in the center and juices run clear, 8 to 10 minutes. Grill the red pepper and onions until tender and golden brown, 8 to 10 minutes. Remove the chicken and vegetables from the grill. Slice the grilled pepper into thin strips.
7. Spread each slice of bread with 1 1/2 teaspoons of prepared lime mayonnaise. Layer half of the pieces of bread with sliced mango, 1 tablespoon prepared salsa, grilled chicken tenderloins, grilled peppers, grilled onions, and a slice of Monterey Jack cheese. Top off the sandwiches with the remaining slices of bread. Return the sandwiches to the grill, turning when the bottom is golden brown
8. Return the sandwiches to the grill and grill them until the bread is toasted and the cheese melts, about 2 minutes per side.

REAL N'AWLINS MUFFULETTA

Servings: 8 | Prep: 40m | Cooks: 0m | Total: 1d | Additional: 1d

NUTRITION FACTS

Calories: 987 | Carbohydrates: 63.2g | Fat: 62.8g | Protein: 41.4g | Cholesterol: 97mg

INGREDIENTS

- 1 cup pimento-stuffed green olives, crushed
- 1 teaspoon dried basil
- 1/2 cup drained kalamata olives, crushed
- 3/4 teaspoon ground black pepper
- 2 cloves garlic, minced
- 1/4 cup red wine vinegar
- 1/4 cup roughly chopped pickled cauliflower florets
- 1/2 cup olive oil
- 2 tablespoons drained capers
- ¼ cup canola oil
- 1 tablespoon chopped celery
- 2 (1 pound) loaves Italian bread
- 1 tablespoon chopped carrot
- 8 ounces thinly sliced Genoa salami
- 1/2 cup pepperoncini, drained
- 8 ounces thinly sliced cooked ham
- 1/4 cup marinated cocktail onions
- 8 ounces sliced mortadella
- 1/2 teaspoon celery seed
- 8 ounces sliced mozzarella cheese
- 1 teaspoon dried oregano

- 8 ounces sliced provolone cheese

DIRECTIONS

1. To Make Olive Salad: In a medium bowl, combine the green olives, kalamata olives, garlic, cauliflower, capers, celery, carrot, pepperoncini, cocktail onions, celery seed, oregano, basil, black pepper, vinegar, olive oil and canola oil. Mix together and transfer mixture into a glass jar (or other nonreactive container). If needed, pour in more oil to cover. Cover jar or container and refrigerate at least overnight.
2. To Make Sandwiches: Cut loaves of bread in half horizontally; hollow out some of the excess bread to make room for filling. Spread each piece of bread with equal amounts olive salad, including oil. Layer 'bottom half' of each loaf with 1/2 of the salami, ham, mortadella, mozzarella and Provolone. Replace 'top half' on each loaf and cut sandwich into quarters.
3. Serve immediately, or wrap tightly and refrigerate for a few hours; this will allow for the flavors to mingle and the olive salad to soak into the bread.

MONTE CRISTO SANDWICH
Servings: 1 | Prep: 5m | Cooks: 15m | Total: 20m

NUTRITION FACTS

Calories: 641 | Carbohydrates: 33.1g | Fat: 33.8g | Protein: 48.7g | Cholesterol: 298mg

INGREDIENTS

- 2 slices bread
- 2 slices cooked turkey meat
- 1 teaspoon mayonnaise
- 1 slice Swiss cheese
- 1 teaspoon prepared mustard
- 1 egg
- 2 slices cooked ham
- 1/2 cup milk

DIRECTIONS

1. Spread bread with mayonnaise and mustard. Alternate ham, Swiss and turkey slices on bread.
2. Beat egg and milk in a small bowl. Coat the sandwich with the egg and milk mixture. Heat a greased skillet over medium heat, brown the sandwich on both sides. Serve hot.

HEARTY MEATBALL SANDWICH
Servings: 6 | Prep: 15m | Cooks: 1h5m | Total: 1h40m | Additional: 20m

Calories: 491 | Carbohydrates: 43.1g | Fat: 21.4g | Protein: 29.3g | Cholesterol: 75mg

INGREDIENTS

- 1 1/2 pounds lean ground beef
- 1 tablespoon cracked black pepper
- 1/3 cup Italian seasoned bread crumbs
- 1 teaspoon garlic powder
- 1/2 small onion, chopped
- 1/2 cup marinara sauce
- 1 teaspoon salt
- 3 hoagie rolls, split lengthwise
- 1/2 cup shredded mozzarella cheese, divided

DIRECTIONS

1. Preheat the oven to 350 degrees F (175 degrees C).
2. In a medium bowl, mix together the ground beef, bread crumbs, onion, salt and pepper, garlic powder, and half of the mozzarella cheese. Form the mixture into a log, and place it into an 8x8 inch baking dish.
3. Bake for 50 minutes in the preheated oven, or until the center is no longer pink. Let stand for 5 minutes, then slice into 1/2 inch slices. Place a few slices onto each hoagie roll, cover with marinara sauce, and sprinkle remaining mozzarella cheese over.
4. Wrap each sandwich with aluminum foil, and return to the oven for 15 minutes, until bread is lightly toasted and cheese is melted. Let stand 15 minutes before eating. Each sandwich serves 2.

SENSATIONAL STEAK SANDWICH
Servings: 4 | Prep: 30m | Cooks: 4h20m | Total: 4h50m

NUTRITION FACTS

Calories: 908 | Carbohydrates: 78.8g | Fat: 40.6g | Protein: 55.7g | Cholesterol: 109mg

INGREDIENTS

- 2 tablespoons olive oil
- 1/2 teaspoon salt
- 1 pound thinly sliced sirloin steak strips
- 1/2 teaspoon ground black pepper
- 8 ounces sliced fresh mushrooms
- 1/2 teaspoon garlic powder
- 1 green bell pepper, seeded and cut into strips

- 2 tablespoons Worcestershire sauce
- 1 medium onion, sliced
- 1/8 teaspoon red pepper flakes
- 10 slices provolone cheese
- 1/4 cup Pinot Noir or other dry red wine
- 1 loaf French bread
- 1/2 cup prepared horseradish (optional)
- 1 (14 ounce) can beef broth
- 1/2 cup brown mustard (optional)

DIRECTIONS

1. Heat the oil in a large skillet over medium heat. Add the beef, and cook until browned. Add the mushrooms, bell pepper and onion; cook and stir until starting to become tender, about 5 minutes.
2. In a slow cooker, combine the beef broth, salt, pepper, Worcestershire sauce, red pepper flakes and red wine. Transfer the beef and vegetables to the slow cooker, and stir to blend. Cover, and cook on High for 3 to 4 hours, until beef is extremely tender.
3. Preheat the oven to 425 degrees F (220 degrees C). Drain the liquid from the slow cooker, and save for dipping. Slice the French bread loaf lengthwise like a submarine sandwich. Mix together the horseradish and mustard; spread onto the inside of the loaf. Place slices of provolone cheese on both sides of the loaf, then fill with the beef and vegetables. Close the loaf, and wrap the entire sandwich with aluminum foil.
4. Bake for 10 to 15 minutes in the preheated oven. For crunchier bread, you can bake it without the aluminum foil. Slice into servings, and serve with the juices from the slow cooker for dipping.

MINI MEATBALL SUBS

Servings: 8 | Prep: 20m | Cooks: 50m | Total: 1h10m

NUTRITION FACTS

Calories: 351 | Carbohydrates: 32.2g | Fat: 16.4g | Protein: 18g | Cholesterol: 68mg

INGREDIENTS

- 1 pound ground beef
- 1 teaspoon seasoned salt
- 1/2 cup chopped onion
- 1 teaspoon ground black pepper
- 1/2 cup chopped green pepper
- 1 (26.5 ounce) can spaghetti sauce
- 1/2 cup crushed butter-flavored crackers
- 1/2 cup shredded mozzarella cheese
- 1 egg

- 1/3 cup grated Parmesan cheese
- 1 teaspoon Worcestershire sauce
- 8 dinner rolls, split
- 1 teaspoon chopped garlic

DIRECTIONS

1. Preheat an oven to 350 degrees F (175 degrees C).
2. Combine ground beef, onion, green pepper, crackers, and egg in a large bowl. Season with Worcestershire sauce, garlic, seasoned salt, and pepper; mix well. Form mixture into 8 meatballs. Place meatballs in a 9x13 inch baking dish.
3. Bake meatballs in the preheated oven for 20 minutes. Pour the spaghetti sauce into a large saucepan; bring to a simmer over low heat. Stir baked meatballs into the simmering sauce. Do not turn oven off. Simmer sauce until meatballs are fully cooked, about 20 minutes.
4. Place one meatball, a sprinkle of mozzarella, a sprinkle of Parmesan, and a bit of sauce between each roll. Place sandwiches in hot oven; bake until cheeses melt, about 7 minutes.

BARBECUE TOFU SANDWICHES
Servings: 6 | Prep: 5m | Cooks: 10m | Total: 15m

NUTRITION FACTS

Calories: 335 | Carbohydrates: 47.1g | Fat: 0g | Protein: 9.4g | Cholesterol: 0mg

INGREDIENTS

- 1 (12 ounce) package extra firm tofu
- 1 1/2 cups barbecue sauce
- 3 tablespoons vegetable oil
- 6 hamburger buns
- 1 onion, thinly sliced

DIRECTIONS

1. Drain the tofu between paper towels until most of the water has been squeezed out.
2. Slice tofu into 1/4 inch thick slices.
3. Heat vegetable oil in a large skillet, fry tofu strips until golden brown on both sides. Add onion and cook for a few minutes, until onion is at your desired consistency.
4. Pour in barbeque sauce (use more or less, according to your taste). Cook the mixture for ten minutes on low and serve on buns.

JALAPENO POPPER GRILLED CHEESE SANDWICH
Servings: 2 | Prep: 10m | Cooks: 10m | Total: 20m

NUTRITION FACTS

Calories: 528 | Carbohydrates: 40.9g | Fat: 34g | Protein: 16.5g | Cholesterol: 89mg

INGREDIENTS

- 2 ounces cream cheese, softened
- 4 teaspoons butter
- 1 tablespoon sour cream
- 8 tortilla chips, crushed
- 10 pickled jalapeno pepper slices, or to taste - chopped
- 1/2 cup shredded Colby-Monterey Jack cheese
- 2 ciabatta sandwich rolls

DIRECTIONS

1. Combine the cream cheese, sour cream, and pickled jalapeno in a small bowl. Set aside. Preheat skillet over medium heat.
2. Slice each roll in half horizontally, then slice the rounded tops off the ciabatta rolls to make a flat top half. Spread 1 teaspoon butter on the doughy cut side of the bottom bun and 1 teaspoon butter on the now flattened top bun. Place half of the cream cheese mixture, half of the crushed chips, and half of the shredded cheese on the non-buttered side of the bottom bun. Place the top half of the bun on the sandwich and place the sandwich on the hot skillet. Repeat with the second sandwich.
3. Grill until lightly browned and flip over, about 3 to 5 minutes; continue grilling until cheese is melted and the second side is golden brown.

EASIEST SLOW COOKER FRENCH DIP
Servings: 8 | Prep: 5m | Cooks: 8h | Total: 8h5m

NUTRITION FACTS

Calories: 756 | Carbohydrates: 70.5g | Fat: 30g | Protein: 46.8g | Cholesterol: 110mg

INGREDIENTS

- 3 pounds beef sirloin roast
- 8 (1 ounce) slices provolone cheese
- 1 (1 ounce) packet dry au jus mix
- 8 hoagie rolls, split lengthwise
- 1 cup water

DIRECTIONS

1. Place the beef roast into a slow cooker. Stir together the water and au jus mix; pour over the roast. Cover and cook on Low for 6 to 8 hours.

2. Remove the roast from the slow cooker and shred or slice. Open the hoagie rolls and top with beef and provolone cheese. Serve with small bowls of the hot au jus from the slow cooker.

LOOSEMEAT SANDWICHES
Servings: 8 | Prep: 20m | Cooks: 40m | Total: 60m

NUTRITION FACTS

Calories: 356 | Carbohydrates: 24.2g | Fat: 16.3g | Protein: 26.6g | Cholesterol: 74mg

INGREDIENTS

- 2 pounds lean ground beef
- 1 onion, chopped
- 1 teaspoon salt
- 24 slices dill pickle slices
- 1/2 teaspoon ground black pepper
- 4 ounces prepared mustard
- 1 1/2 cups water
- 8 hamburger buns

DIRECTIONS

1. In a large skillet over medium heat, cook the ground beef until brown. Drain. Return to pan with salt, pepper, and water to cover. Reduce heat to low and simmer, uncovered, until water is gone, 15 to 30 minutes.
2. Serve meat on buns topped with chopped onion, dill pickle slices and mustard.

GRILLED APPLE AND SWISS CHEESE SANDWICH
Servings: 1 | Prep: 10m | Cooks: 5m | Total: 15m

NUTRITION FACTS

Calories: 371 | Carbohydrates: 33.9g | Fat: 19g | Protein: 17.3g | Cholesterol: 33mg

INGREDIENTS

- 2 slices whole wheat bread
- 1 1/2 teaspoons olive oil
- 1/2 Granny Smith apple - peeled, cored and thinly sliced
- 1/3 cup shredded Swiss cheese

DIRECTIONS

1. Preheat a skillet over medium heat. Lightly brush one side of each slice of bread with the olive oil. Place 1 slice of bread, olive oil side down into the skillet, and arrange the apple slices evenly over the top. Sprinkle the Swiss cheese over the apple, then top with the remaining slice of bread, olive oil-side up. Cook until the bread is golden brown, then flip the sandwich over, and cook until the other side is golden brown and the cheese has melted, 1 to 2 more minutes.

CALIFORNIA MELT
Servings: 8 | Prep: 15m | Cooks: 2m | Total: 17m

NUTRITION FACTS

Calories: 335 | Carbohydrates: 21.1g | Fat: 22.5g | Protein: 15.6g | Cholesterol: 26mg

INGREDIENTS

- 4 slices whole-grain bread, lightly toasted
- 1/3 cup sliced toasted almonds
- 1 avocado, sliced
- 1 tomato, sliced
- 1 cup sliced mushrooms
- 4 slices Swiss cheese

DIRECTIONS

1. Preheat the oven broiler.
2. Lay the toasted bread out on a baking sheet. Top each slice of bread with 1/4 of the avocado, mushrooms, almonds, and tomato slices. Top each with a slice of Swiss cheese.
3. Broil the open-face sandwiches until the cheese melts and begins to bubble, about 2 minutes. Serve the sandwiches warm.

CLASSIC CUBAN MIDNIGHT (MEDIANOCHE) SANDWICH
Servings: 4 | Prep: 15m | Cooks: 8m | Total: 23m

NUTRITION FACTS

Calories: 1453 | Carbohydrates: 69.1g | Fat: 88.4g | Protein: 92.1g | Cholesterol: 275mg

INGREDIENTS

- 4 sweet bread rolls
- 1 pound thinly sliced fully cooked pork
- 1/2 cup mayonnaise
- 1 pound sliced Swiss cheese
- 1/4 cup prepared mustard

- 1 cup dill pickle slices
- 1 pound thinly sliced cooked ham
- 2 tablespoons butter, melted

DIRECTIONS

1. Split the sandwich rolls in half, and spread mustard and mayonnaise liberally onto the cut sides. On each sandwich, place and equal amount of Swiss cheese, ham and pork in exactly that order. Place a few pickles onto each one, and put the top of the roll onto the sandwich. Brush the tops with melted butter.
2. Press each sandwich in a sandwich press heated to medium-high heat. If a sandwich press is not available, use a large skillet over medium-high heat, and press the sandwiches down using a sturdy plate or skillet. Some indoor grills may be good for this also. Cook for 5 to 8 minutes, keeping sandwiches pressed. If using a skillet, you may want to flip them once for even browning. Slice diagonally and serve hot.

EASY CHICKEN GYRO

Servings: 6 | Prep: 20m | Cooks: 20m | Total: 1h45m | Additional: 1h5m

NUTRITION FACTS

Calories: 441.1 | Carbohydrates: 39.3g | Fat: 0g | Protein: 30.3g | Cholesterol: 70.8mg

INGREDIENTS

- 1 (16 ounce) container Greek yogurt
- 2 teaspoons red wine vinegar
- 1 cucumber, peeled and coarsely chopped
- 2 tablespoons extra-virgin olive oil
- 1 1/2 teaspoons dried dill weed
- 1 tablespoon dried oregano
- 2 cloves garlic, minced
- 1 1/4 pounds skinless, boneless chicken breast halves - cut into strips
- 1 teaspoon distilled white vinegar
- 6 (6 inch) pita bread rounds
- 1 teaspoon lemon juice
- 1 teaspoon olive oil
- 1 tablespoon extra-virgin olive oil
- 1 tomato, diced
- 1 pinch salt and ground black pepper to taste
- 1 red onion, thinly sliced
- 4 cloves garlic, minced
- 1/2 head iceberg lettuce, chopped

- 1 lemon, juiced

DIRECTIONS

1. Place Greek yogurt, cucumber, dill weed, 2 cloves garlic, white vinegar, 1 teaspoon lemon juice, 1 tablespoon olive oil, salt, and black pepper in a blender. Blend until smooth; set aside.
2. Whisk together 4 cloves minced garlic, juice of 1 lemon, red wine vinegar, 2 tablespoons olive oil, and oregano in a large glass or ceramic bowl. Season to taste with salt and black pepper.
3. Stir in chicken strips and toss to evenly coat. Cover the bowl with plastic wrap and marinate in the refrigerator for 1 hour.
4. Preheat the oven's broiler and set the oven rack about 6 inches from the heat source.
5. Remove chicken from the marinade and shake off excess. Discard the remaining marinade. Place chicken on a large baking sheet.
6. Broil the chicken in the preheated oven until lightly browned and no longer pink in the center, 2 to 4 minutes per side.
7. Transfer cooked chicken to a plate and allow to rest for 5 minutes.
8. Heat 1 teaspoon olive oil in a large skillet over medium heat; place each pita bread into the skillet until warm and soft, about 2 minutes per pita.
9. Serve warmed pita bread topped with chicken strips, yogurt sauce, tomatoes, onion, and lettuce.

SEATTLE CREAM CHEESE DOGS
Servings: 4 | Prep: 10m | Cooks: 20m | Total: 30m

NUTRITION FACTS

Calories: 533 | Carbohydrates: 28.8g | Fat: 40.6g | Protein: 13.8g | Cholesterol: 92mg

INGREDIENTS

- 1/4 cup butter
- 4 hot dog buns
- 1 Walla Walla or other sweet onion, thinly sliced
- brown mustard
- 1 (4 ounce) package cream cheese
- sauerkraut (optional)
- 4 hot dogs, or your favorite sausages

DIRECTIONS

1. Preheat grill or grill pan for medium-high heat.
2. Melt butter in a skillet over medium heat. Add onions, and cook slowly until the onions have softened and turned deep brown, about 15 minutes. Warm the cream cheese over low heat in a small skillet until very soft.
3. Grill hot dogs until well browned. Lightly grill hot dog buns on both sides.

4. To assemble cheese dogs, spread warm cream cheese on toasted hot dog bun, add hot dog or sausage, top with onions, mustard and sauerkraut, if desired.

QUEENIE'S KILLER TOMATO BAGEL SANDWICH
Servings: 1 | Prep: 10m | Cooks: 0m | Total: 10m

NUTRITION FACTS

Calories: 358 | Carbohydrates: 50.8g | Fat: 11.7g | Protein: 12.1g | Cholesterol: 32mg

INGREDIENTS

- 1 bagel, split and toasted
- salt and pepper to taste
- 2 tablespoons cream cheese
- 4 leaves fresh basil
- 1 roma (plum) tomatoes, thinly sliced

DIRECTIONS

1. Spread cream cheese on bagel halves. Top cream cheese with tomato slices. Sprinkle with salt and pepper. Top with fresh basil leaves.

TONYA'S TERRIFIC SLOPPY JOES
Servings: 8 | Prep: 10m | Cooks: 30m | Total: 40m

NUTRITION FACTS

Calories: 362 | Carbohydrates: 31.2g | Fat: 15.3g | Protein: 23.7g | Cholesterol: 71mg

INGREDIENTS

- 2 pounds ground beef
- 1 1/2 teaspoons Worcestershire sauce
- 1/2 cup chopped onion
- 1 teaspoon vinegar
- 1/4 cup chopped celery
- 1/4 teaspoon dry mustard powder
- 7 ounces ketchup
- 1/8 teaspoon lemon juice
- 1 tablespoon brown sugar
- 8 white or wheat hamburger buns

DIRECTIONS

1. Place a large skillet over medium-high heat. Crumble ground beef into skillet; add onion and celery. Cook and stir beef mixture until beef is completely browned, 7 to 10 minutes.
2. Stir ketchup, brown sugar, Worcestershire sauce, vinegar, mustard, and lemon juice through the beef mixture. Reduce heat to medium-low and cook mixture at a simmer until mixture is hot and sauce has thickened, about 20 minutes.

BBQ CHICKEN SANDWICHES
Servings: 12 | Prep: 15m | Cooks: 4h | Total: 4h15m

NUTRITION FACTS

Calories: 662.1 | Carbohydrates: 51.4g | Fat: 0g | Protein: 47.9g | Cholesterol: 136.8mg

INGREDIENTS

- 2 (4 pound) whole chickens, cut up
- 1/4 cup steak sauce
- 1 1/2 cups ketchup
- 4 tablespoons lemon juice
- 3/4 cup prepared mustard
- 3 tablespoons liquid smoke flavoring
- 5 tablespoons brown sugar
- salt and pepper to taste
- 5 tablespoons minced garlic
- 12 hamburger buns
- 5 tablespoons honey
- 3 cups prepared coleslaw

DIRECTIONS

1. Place chicken in a large pot with enough water to cover. Bring to a boil, and cook until chicken comes off the bone easily, about 3 hours. Make sauce while the chicken cooks
2. In a saucepan over medium heat, mix together the ketchup, mustard, brown sugar, garlic, honey, steak sauce, lemon juice, and liquid smoke. Season with salt and pepper. Bring to a gentle boil, and simmer for about 10 minutes. Set aside to allow flavors to mingle.
3. When the chicken is done, remove all meat from the bones, and chop or shred into small pieces. Place in a pan with the sauce, and cook for about 15 minutes to let the flavor of the sauce soak into the chicken. Spoon barbequed chicken onto buns, and top with coleslaw if you like.

GRILLED MEDITERRANEAN VEGETABLE SANDWICH
Servings: 6 | Prep: 20m | Cooks: 40m | Total: 3h

NUTRITION FACTS

Calories: 356 | Carbohydrates: 48.3g | Fat: 14.8g | Protein: 9g | Cholesterol: 3mg

INGREDIENTS

- 1 eggplant, sliced into strips
- 3 cloves garlic, crushed
- 2 red bell peppers
- 4 tablespoons mayonnaise
- 2 tablespoons olive oil, divided
- 1 (1 pound) loaf focaccia bread
- 2 portobello mushrooms, sliced

DIRECTIONS

1. Preheat oven to 400 degrees F (200 degrees C).
2. Brush eggplant and red bell peppers with 1 tablespoon olive oil; use more if necessary, depending on sizes of vegetables. Place on a baking sheet and roast in preheated oven. Roast eggplant until tender, about 25 minutes; roast peppers until blackened. Remove from oven and set aside to cool.
3. Meanwhile, heat 1 tablespoon olive oil and cook and stir mushrooms until tender. Stir crushed garlic into mayonnaise. Slice focaccia in half lengthwise. Spread mayonnaise mixture on one or both halves.
4. Peel cooled peppers, core, and slice. Arrange eggplant, peppers and mushrooms on focaccia. Wrap sandwich in plastic wrap; place a cutting board on top of it and weight it down with some canned foods. Allow sandwich to sit for 2 hours before slicing and serving.

SASSY TAILGATE SANDWICHES

Servings: 12 | Prep: 35m | Cooks: 25m | Total: 1h

NUTRITION FACTS

Calories: 585 | Carbohydrates: 44.7g | Fat: 26.6g | Protein: 30.8g | Cholesterol: 138mg

INGREDIENTS

- 1 (12 count) package Hawaiian bread rolls
- 1/2 cup butter, melted
- 1 pound shaved Black Forest ham
- 1 tablespoon Worcestershire sauce
- 12 slices Gruyere cheese
- 1/2 tablespoon dried minced onion
- 1 (8 ounce) tub PHILADELPHIA Chive & Onion Cream Cheese Spread
- 1/4 cup grated Parmesan cheese

DIRECTIONS

1. Cut all rolls in half. Place roll bottoms in 9x13-inch pan.
2. Place equal amounts of ham on each roll bottom. Top with Gruyere.
3. On each of the roll tops, spread a generous amount of the cream cheese spread. Return the tops to the bottoms making sandwiches.
4. In a separate bowl, mix together the butter, Worcestershire sauce, onion and Parmesan cheese. Pour over your sandwiches and let sit for at least 20 minutes. (You can make these ahead of time and allow to sit in fridge overnight.)
5. Place sandwiches, covered in foil, in a preheated 350 degrees F oven. Bake for 20 minutes or until warmed through. Enjoy.

BREAKFAST ROUNDS

Servings: 8 | Prep: 10m | Cooks: 3m | Total: 13m

NUTRITION FACTS

Calories: 219 | Carbohydrates: 25.2g | Fat: 11.3g | Protein: 6.4g | Cholesterol: 0mg

INGREDIENTS

- 1/2 cup peanut butter
- 1/4 cup packed brown sugar
- 4 English muffins, split and toasted
- 2 tablespoons margarine
- 1 red apple, cored and sliced
- 1/4 teaspoon ground cinnamon

DIRECTIONS

1. Spread 1 tablespoon of peanut butter onto each English muffin half. Top each one with a few apple slices. In the microwave, melt together the brown sugar, margarine and cinnamon, stirring frequently until smooth. Drizzle the cinnamon mixture over apple slices. Mmmmmm...

BARBEQUE TEMPEH SANDWICHES

Servings: 4 | Prep: 10m | Cooks: 15m | Total: 25m

NUTRITION FACTS

Calories: 375 | Carbohydrates: 54.7g | Fat: 11.5g | Protein: 15.2g | Cholesterol: 0mg

INGREDIENTS

- 1 cup barbecue sauce, your choice
- 1 green bell pepper, seeded and chopped
- 1 (8 ounce) package tempeh, crumbled
- 1 medium onion, chopped

- 1 tablespoon vegetable oil
- 4 kaiser rolls, split and toasted
- 1 red bell pepper, seeded and chopped

DIRECTIONS

1. Pour the barbeque sauce into a medium bowl. Crumble the tempeh into the sauce, and let it marinate a little, about 10 minutes.
2. Heat oil in a skillet over medium heat. Add the red and green peppers, and the onion. Cook, stirring frequently until tender. Stir in the tempeh and barbeque sauce, and heat through.
3. Spoon the tempeh mixture onto kaiser rolls, and serve.

TURKEY SLOPPY JOES

Servings: 8 | Prep: 15m | Cooks: 15m | Total: 30m

NUTRITION FACTS

Calories: 393 | Carbohydrates: 36.4g | Fat: 13.3g | Protein: 32.8g | Cholesterol: 105mg

INGREDIENTS

- 2 1/2 pounds ground turkey
- 2 tablespoons prepared yellow mustard
- 1/2 cup chopped onion
- 1 tablespoon vinegar
- 1/2 cup chopped green bell pepper
- 1/2 teaspoon celery seed
- 1/2 cup chopped tomato
- 1/2 teaspoon ground black pepper
- 1 cup no-salt-added ketchup
- 1/2 teaspoon red pepper flakes, or to taste
- 7 tablespoons barbeque sauce
- 8 hamburger bun, split and toasted

DIRECTIONS

1. Heat a nonstick skillet over medium heat; cook and stir turkey, onion, bell pepper, and tomato until turkey is crumbly and no longer pink, about 5 minutes. Stir in ketchup, barbeque sauce, mustard, vinegar, celery seed, black pepper, and red pepper flakes. Reduce heat to low and simmer for 10 minutes, stirring occasionally. Serve turkey mixture on toasted hamburger buns.

SIMPLE TUNA MELT

Servings: 1 | Prep: 3m | Cooks: 7m | Total: 10m

NUTRITION FACTS

Calories: 608 | Carbohydrates: 26.8g | Fat: 34.2g | Protein: 46.8g | Cholesterol: 78mg

INGREDIENTS

- 1 (5 ounce) can tuna, drained and flaked
- 1 teaspoon Dijon mustard
- 2 tablespoons mayonnaise
- 2 slices whole wheat bread
- 1 pinch salt
- 2 teaspoons chopped dill pickle
- 1 teaspoon balsamic vinegar
- 1/4 cup shredded sharp Cheddar cheese

DIRECTIONS

1. Preheat the oven to 375 degrees F (190 degrees C). Place bread slices in the oven to toast while it preheats, and while you make the tuna salad.
2. In a small bowl, mix together the tuna, mayonnaise, salt, balsamic vinegar, mustard and dill pickle until well blended. Remove bread from the oven, and pile the tuna mixture onto one slice. Sprinkle cheese over the other slice of bread.
3. Bake for 7 minutes in the preheated oven, or until cheese is melted and tuna is heated through. Place the cheese side of the sandwich on top of the tuna side. Cut in half and serve immediately.

REUBEN SANDWICH

Servings: 4 | Prep: 15m | Cooks: 10m | Total: 25m

NUTRITION FACTS

Calories: 793 | Carbohydrates: 50.2g | Fat: 51.7g | Protein: 34.2g | Cholesterol: 107mg

INGREDIENTS

- 8 slices rye bread
- 8 slices Swiss cheese
- 3/4 cup thousand island dressing
- 8 slices pastrami
- 1 (16 ounce) can sauerkraut, drained
- 1/2 cup margarine, softened

DIRECTIONS

1. Spread each slice of bread with thousand island dressing. Top 4 of the bread slices with sauerkraut, cheese and pastrami. Place remaining bread slices on sandwich. Spread margarine on the outsides of each sandwich.
2. Heat a large skillet over medium high heat. Grill until browned, then turn and grill until heated through, and cheese is melted.

LOOSE MEAT ON A BUN, RESTAURANT STYLE
Servings: 12 | Prep: 10m | Cooks: 50m | Total: 1h15m | Additional: 15m

NUTRITION FACTS

Calories: 341 | Carbohydrates: 22.9g | Fat: 16.4g | Protein: 23.6g | Cholesterol: 71mg

INGREDIENTS

- 3 pounds ground beef
- 1 teaspoon salt
- 1/4 cup minced onion
- 1 teaspoon ground black pepper
- 3 tablespoons Worcestershire sauce
- 2 teaspoons butter
- 4 cups beef broth
- 12 hamburger buns, split

DIRECTIONS

1. Crumble the ground beef and onion into a large skillet over medium-high heat. Cook, stirring to break up lumps, until no longer pink. Drain off the grease and return to the stove. Add the Worcestershire sauce, beef broth, salt, pepper, and butter. Bring to a boil, then set the heat to low and simmer uncovered until the liquid is almost completely gone, about 40 minutes. Remove from the heat, cover, and let rest for 15 minutes before serving on buns.

EGGPLANT AND PEPPER PARMESAN SANDWICHES
Servings: 4 | Prep: 15m | Cooks: 10m | Total: 25m

NUTRITION FACTS

Calories: 461 | Carbohydrates: 74.7g | Fat: 9.6g | Protein: 20.3g | Cholesterol: 13mg

INGREDIENTS

- 1 eggplant, seeded and cut lengthwise into 1/4 inch slices
- 2 ounces soft goat cheese
- 1 red bell pepper, sliced into thin strips

- 1/4 cup tapenade (olive spread)
- salt and pepper to taste
- 1/4 cup grated Parmesan cheese
- 1 French baguette

DIRECTIONS

1. Preheat the oven broiler.
2. Place the eggplant and red bell pepper on a medium baking sheet, and season with salt and pepper. Broil 5 to 10 minutes, until tender and slightly browned.
3. Cut baguette in half lengthwise. Spread bottom half with goat cheese, followed by tapenade. Layer with eggplant and red pepper, then sprinkle with Parmesan cheese. Cover with top half of baguette. Cut into 4 pieces. Serve hot or cold.

BASIL, TOMATO AND MOZZARELLA SANDWICH
Servings: 4 | Prep: 15m | Cooks: 0m | Total: 15m

NUTRITION FACTS

Calories: 421 | Carbohydrates: 64.7g | Fat: 10.3g | Protein: 16g | Cholesterol: 22mg

INGREDIENTS

- 1 (1 pound) loaf Italian bread
- 4 ounces fresh mozzarella cheese, sliced
- 6 fresh basil leaves, chopped
- 1/8 teaspoon red pepper flakes
- 2 tomatoes, sliced
- 1/2 cup balsamic vinegar

DIRECTIONS

1. Slice the loaf of bread in half lengthwise. Layer the basil, tomato slices, and mozzarella cheese between the two halves of bread. Cut into four sandwiches.
2. In a small dish, stir together the balsamic vinegar and red pepper flakes. Use as a dipping sauce.

PICADILLO
Servings: 6 | Prep: 15m | Cooks: 40m | Total: 55m

NUTRITION FACTS

Calories: 486 | Carbohydrates: 22.6g | Fat: 32.7g | Protein: 25.5g | Cholesterol: 79mg

INGREDIENTS

- 2 tablespoons olive oil
- 1/4 teaspoon ground cinnamon
- 1 pound ground beef
- 1 1/2 cups canned diced tomatoes
- 1/2 pound chorizo sausage, chopped
- 3/4 cup beef stock
- 1 large onion, chopped
- 1 tablespoon white sugar
- 1/2 cup chopped red bell pepper
- 1/2 cup raisins
- 2 cloves garlic, chopped
- 1/4 cup chopped pimento-stuffed green olives
- 1 tablespoon ground cumin
- 2 tablespoons apple cider vinegar
- 2 teaspoons chili powder
- 1 tablespoon capers, drained
- 1 teaspoon dried oregano
- 1/3 cup slivered almonds, toasted
- 1 teaspoon paprika
- 1 tablespoon lime juice
- 1/4 teaspoon cayenne pepper

DIRECTIONS

1. Heat the olive oil in a large skillet over medium heat. Add the ground beef and chorizo sausage. Cook and stir until no longer pink, about 10 minutes.
2. Drain off some of the grease, and stir in the onions and bell pepper. Cook until soft, then add the garlic. Season with cumin, chili powder, oregano, paprika, cayenne and cinnamon. Cook and stir for about one minute to release the fragrance. Pour the tomatoes and beef stock into the pan, along with the sugar. Set the heat to low, cover, and simmer for 20 to 30 minutes.
3. Stir the raisins, olives, capers and vinegar into the pan, and simmer uncovered for 5 minutes. Add the almonds and lime juice, and cook until they are heated, then serve.

GOURMET GRILLED CHEESE SANDWICHES
Servings: 4 | Prep: 12m | Cooks: 8m | Total: 20m

NUTRITION FACTS

Calories: 783 | Carbohydrates: 32g | Fat: 64.9g | Protein: 20.6g | Cholesterol: 109mg

INGREDIENTS

- 1 (3 ounce) package cream cheese

- 3/4 teaspoon garlic salt
- 3/4 cup mayonnaise
- 8 slices French bread
- 8 ounces shredded Colby-Monterey Jack cheese
- 2 tablespoons butter

DIRECTIONS

1. In a medium bowl, combine cream cheese, mayonnaise, shredded cheese and garlic salt. Beat until smooth.
2. Preheat a large skillet over medium heat. Spread cheese mixture on 4 slices of bread, then top with the other 4 bread slices. Lightly butter both sides of each sandwich. Place sandwiches in skillet, and grill until golden brown on both sides, about 4 minutes per side.

BARBECUE BEEF FOR SANDWICHES
Servings: 16 | Prep: 5m | Cooks: 2h45m | Total: 2h50m

NUTRITION FACTS

Calories: 200 | Carbohydrates: 4.9g | Fat: 13.3g | Protein: 14.4g | Cholesterol: 53mg

INGREDIENTS

- 4 pounds boneless chuck roast
- 1 teaspoon mustard powder
- 1 onion, chopped
- 2 tablespoons Worcestershire sauce
- 2 tablespoons butter
- 1/2 teaspoon freshly ground black pepper
- 3 tablespoons distilled white vinegar
- 1 teaspoon salt
- 12 ounces chile sauce
- 1/8 teaspoon ground cayenne pepper
- 2 tablespoons brown sugar
- 3 cloves garlic, minced

DIRECTIONS

1. Place roast in a large covered pan. Roast at 325 degrees F (165 degrees C) for 2 hours, or until the meat falls apart and shreds easily.
2. In a large skillet, melt butter over medium heat. Add onions, and saute until onions become translucent.

3. Stir in vinegar and chili sauce. Fill empty chili sauce bottle with water, shake, and pour liquid into skillet. Mix in brown sugar, mustard, Worcestershire sauce, black pepper, salt, cayenne pepper, and garlic. Cook sauce over low heat, stirring often, until thickened.
4. With two forks, shred roasted beef. Stir meat into the sauce in the skillet, and simmer for 30 minutes.

ITALIAN SUBS - RESTAURANT STYLE
Servings: 8 | Prep: 20m | Cooks: 1h | Total: 1h20m | Additional: 1h

NUTRITION FACTS

Calories: 708 | Carbohydrates: 40.4g | Fat: 47.3g | Protein: 29.2g | Cholesterol: 79mg

INGREDIENTS

- 1 head red leaf lettuce, rinsed and torn
- 1/4 teaspoon red pepper flakes
- 2 medium fresh tomatoes, chopped
- 1 pinch dried oregano
- 1 medium red onion, chopped
- 1/2 pound sliced Capacola sausage
- 6 tablespoons olive oil
- 1/2 pound thinly sliced Genoa salami
- 2 tablespoons white wine vinegar
- 1/4 pound thinly sliced prosciutto
- 2 tablespoons chopped fresh parsley
- 1/2 pound sliced provolone cheese
- 2 cloves garlic, chopped
- 4 submarine rolls, split
- 1 teaspoon dried basil
- 1 cup dill pickle slices

DIRECTIONS

1. In a large bowl, toss together the lettuce, tomatoes and onion. In a separate bowl, whisk together the olive oil, white wine vinegar, parsley, garlic, basil, red pepper flakes and oregano. Pour over the salad, and toss to coat evenly. Refrigerate for about 1 hour.
2. Spread the submarine rolls open, and layer the Capacola, salami, prosciutto, and provolone cheese evenly on each roll. Top with some of the salad, and as many pickle slices as desired. Close the rolls and serve.

HOT SHREDDED CHICKEN SANDWICHES
Servings: 12 | Prep: 5m | Cooks: 20m | Total: 25m

Calories: 367.2 | Carbohydrates: 30.6g | Fat: 0g | Protein: 22.5g | Cholesterol: 56.2mg

INGREDIENTS

- 1 (3 pound) chicken - cooked, deboned and shredded
- 1/4 (16 ounce) package buttery round crackers, crushed
- 2 (10.75 ounce) cans condensed cream of mushroom soup
- 12 hamburger buns
- 1/2 teaspoon poultry seasoning

DIRECTIONS

1. In a large saucepan over medium heat, combine shredded chicken, condensed soup, poultry seasoning and crushed crackers. Cook, stirring frequently, until mixture is hot, 15 to 20 minutes. Serve on buns.

SLOPPY JOE SANDWICHES

Servings: 2 | Prep: 5m | Cooks: 40m | Total: 45m

NUTRITION FACTS

Calories: 467 | Carbohydrates: 47.8g | Fat: 20.3g | Protein: 24g | Cholesterol: 69mg

INGREDIENTS

- 1/2 pound ground beef
- 1 teaspoon white vinegar
- 1/2 onion, chopped
- 1 teaspoon chili powder
- 1/2 cup ketchup
- 1/4 teaspoon garlic powder
- 2 tablespoons water
- 1/4 teaspoon onion powder
- 1 tablespoon brown sugar
- 1/4 teaspoon salt
- 1 teaspoon Worcestershire sauce
- 2 hamburger buns, split
- 1 teaspoon prepared mustard

DIRECTIONS

1. Heat a large skillet over medium-high heat and stir in ground beef and onion. Cook and stir until beef is crumbly, evenly browned, and no longer pink, about 10 minutes. Drain and discard any

excess grease. Stir in ketchup, water, brown sugar, Worcestershire sauce, mustard, vinegar, chili powder, garlic powder, onion powder, and salt.

2. Bring beef mixture to a boil over high heat. Reduce heat to low; cover and simmer until sauce has thickened, 30 to 40 minutes. Serve on buns.

HAM BROCCOLI BRAID

Servings: 9 | Prep: 20m | Cooks: 25m | Total: 45m

NUTRITION FACTS

Calories: 3484 | Carbohydrates: 22.8g | Fat: 0g | Protein: 14.4g | Cholesterol: 33.4mg

INGREDIENTS

- 2 cups cooked ham, chopped
- 2 tablespoons Dijon mustard
- 1 cup chopped fresh broccoli
- 1 1/2 cups shredded Swiss cheese
- 1 small onion, chopped
- 2 (8 ounce) cans refrigerated crescent roll dough
- 1 tablespoon dried parsley

DIRECTIONS

1. Preheat oven to 350 degrees F (175 degrees C).
2. In a large bowl, combine ham, broccoli, onion, parsley, mustard and cheese. Stir well.
3. Unroll crescent roll dough, and arrange flat on a medium baking sheet. Pinch together perforations to form a single sheet of dough. Using a knife or scissors, cut 1 inch wide strips in towards the center, starting on the long sides. There should be a solid strip about 3 inches wide down the center, with the cut strips forming a fringe down each side. Spread the filling along the center strip. Fold the side strips over filling, alternating strips from each side. Pinch or twist to seal.
4. Bake in preheated oven for 20 to 25 minutes, until deep golden brown.

THE BEST VEGGIE SANDWICH

Servings: 4 | Prep: 20m | Cooks: 5m | Total: 25m

NUTRITION FACTS

Calories: 470 | Carbohydrates: 37.1g | Fat: 30.2g | Protein: 15.8g | Cholesterol: 34mg

INGREDIENTS

- 4 English muffins, split and toasted
- 1 small sweet onion, chopped

- 1 avocado, mashed
- 4 tablespoons Ranch-style salad dressing
- 1 cup alfalfa sprouts
- 4 tablespoons toasted sesame seeds
- 1 small tomato, chopped
- 1 cup shredded smoked Cheddar cheese

DIRECTIONS

1. Preheat oven to broil.
2. Place each muffin open-faced on a cookie sheet. Spread each half with mashed avocado; place halves close together. Distributing ingredients evenly, cover each half with sprouts, tomatoes, onion, dressing, sesame seeds and cheese.
3. Place under broiler for about 5 minutes, or until cheese is melted and bubbly.

GYROLL

Servings: 4 | Prep: 25m | Cooks: 35m | Total: 1h

NUTRITION FACTS

Calories: 694 | Carbohydrates: 66.6g | Fat: 32.9g | Protein: 32.5g | Cholesterol: 95mg

INGREDIENTS

- 1 tablespoon olive oil
- 1 dash hot pepper sauce
- 1 pound ground lamb
- 2/3 cup chopped fresh parsley
- 6 cloves garlic, crushed
- 1 pound pizza crust dough
- 1 large onion, sliced
- 6 ounces feta cheese
- 1 tablespoon dried oregano
- 1/2 zucchini, diced
- 2/3 teaspoon ground cumin
- 8 ounces chopped black olives
- 2 teaspoons salt
- 1/2 teaspoon garlic powder
- 2 teaspoons freshly ground black pepper

DIRECTIONS

1. Preheat oven to 450 degrees F (230 degrees C).

2. Heat oil in a large skillet over medium-high heat. Brown meat with garlic, onion, oregano, cumin, salt, pepper and hot pepper sauce. When meat is almost done, add parsley and cook until the parsley wilts. Remove mixture from heat and allow to cool.
3. Roll pizza dough out into a rectangle (about 18 inches by 12 inches), with the long side laid out left-to-right in front of you. Spread out feta cheese, zucchini and black olives evenly over the dough, leaving 3 inches from the edges of the crust uncovered. Spread the cooled meat mixture over the top, still leaving edges of dough uncovered.
4. Starting with the edge closest to you, roll up the whole thing until it is all rolled up. You can do this by using the uncovered edge of dough at the end as a 'strip' to stick to the roll and seal it, making sure both ends are pressed down and sealed. Sprinkle with garlic powder and bake in the preheated oven for 5 minutes. Then, reduce heat to 350 degrees F (175 degrees C) and bake for about 30 minutes, or until golden brown.

BLT
Servings: 1 | Prep: 5m | Cooks: 10m | Total: 15m

NUTRITION FACTS

Calories: 439 | Carbohydrates: 28.8g | Fat: 27.8g | Protein: 17.9g | Cholesterol: 45mg

INGREDIENTS

- 4 slices bacon
- 2 slices bread, toasted
- 2 leaves lettuce
- 1 tablespoon mayonnaise
- 2 slices tomato

DIRECTIONS

1. Cook the bacon in a large, deep skillet over medium-high heat until evenly browned, about 10 minutes. Drain the bacon slices on a paper towel-lined plate.
2. Arrange the cooked bacon, lettuce, and tomato slices on one slice of bread. Spread one side of remaining bread slice with the mayonnaise. Bring the two pieces together to make a sandwich.

MOMMA'S SLOPPY JOES
Servings: 6 | Prep: 15m | Cooks: 40m | Total: 55m

NUTRITION FACTS

Calories: 170 | Carbohydrates: 14.5g | Fat: 6g | Protein: 15.9g | Cholesterol: 56mg

INGREDIENTS

- 1 pound ground turkey
- 2 tablespoons white vinegar
- 1 cup ketchup
- 2 tablespoons yellow mustard
- 2 tablespoons white sugar

DIRECTIONS

1. Place the turkey in a large skillet over medium heat, cook until evenly brown, and drain.
2. In a large saucepan over medium heat, mix the ketchup, sugar, vinegar, and mustard. Mix in the turkey. Cook, stirring often, 30 minutes.

HARVEY HAM SANDWICHES

Servings: 24 | Prep: 30m | Cooks: 10h | Total: 10h30m

NUTRITION FACTS

Calories: 445 | Carbohydrates: 33.9g | Fat: 23.2g | Protein: 24.5g | Cholesterol: 65mg

INGREDIENTS

- 1 (6 pound) bone-in ham
- 1 pound brown sugar
- 1 (8 ounce) jar yellow mustard
- 24 dinner rolls, split

DIRECTIONS

1. Place the ham in a large pot or slow cooker, and fill with enough water to cover. Bring to a boil, then reduce the heat to low, and simmer for 8 to 10 hours. Remove the meat from the water, and allow to cool. If it has cooked long enough, it will fall into pieces as you pick it up.
2. Pull the ham apart into shreds once it is cool enough to handle. It doesn't have to be tiny shreds. Place the shredded ham into a slow cooker. Stir in the mustard and brown sugar, cover, and set to Low. Cook just until heated. Serve on dinner rolls. We don't use any other sandwich toppings with it, but that is a personal choice.

FAYE'S PULLED BARBECUE PORK

Servings: 11 | Prep: 10m | Cooks: 3h30m | Total: 3h40m

NUTRITION FACTS

Calories: 694 | Carbohydrates: 26.5g | Fat: 44.8g | Protein: 42.8g | Cholesterol: 176mg

INGREDIENTS

- 6 pounds Boston butt roast
- 1/8 tablespoon cayenne pepper
- 4 cloves garlic, minced
- 1 onion, chopped
- 2 teaspoons seasoning salt
- 3 cups barbecue sauce
- 2 teaspoons ground black pepper

DIRECTIONS

1. Rub garlic, seasoning salt, pepper and cayenne pepper to taste onto roast.
2. Place roast in a large Dutch oven and fill half way with water; add onion. Bring to a rolling boil over high heat. Reduce heat simmer and let cook until meat falls off the bone. This should take at least 3 to 4 hours depending on the size of the roast.
3. Place hot roast in a serving bowl and pour on your favorite barbecue sauce. Stir until well blended. Serve on your favorite buns.

ULTIMATE STEAK SANDWICH
Servings: 4 | Prep: 15m | Cooks: 15m | Total: 30m

NUTRITION FACTS

Calories: 949 | Carbohydrates: 27.7g | Fat: 62.9g | Protein: 65.9g | Cholesterol: 171mg

INGREDIENTS

- 4 hard rolls, split
- 1 large onion, sliced and quartered
- 1/2 cup mayonnaise
- 1 pinch coarse sea salt
- 3 cloves garlic, minced
- 1/2 teaspoon Worcestershire sauce
- 1 tablespoon Parmesan cheese
- 1/8 teaspoon liquid smoke
- 3 tablespoons olive oil
- 8 (1 ounce) slices provolone cheese
- 2 pounds round steak, thinly sliced
- 1/2 teaspoon Italian seasoning

DIRECTIONS

1. Preheat an oven to 500 degrees F (260 degrees C). Split the rolls open and toast them on a baking sheet in the oven while it is preheating. Mix together the mayonnaise, garlic, and Parmesan cheese in a small bowl. Refrigerate until ready to use. Remove the rolls from the oven when toasted as desired.

2. Heat olive oil in a large skillet over medium-high heat. Carefully place the sliced steak and onions in the pan and season with sea salt, Worcestershire sauce, and liquid smoke. Cook and stir until the steak is browned and the onion is tender, about 10 minutes.
3. Generously spread the prepared garlic-Parmesan mayonnaise on both halves of the toasted rolls. Divide the steak and onion mixture evenly among the bottom halves of the rolls, piling them high. Top each with 2 slices provolone cheese and sprinkle with Italian seasoning. Place the tops on the sandwiches.
4. Bake the sandwiches on a baking sheet in the preheated oven until the cheese is melted, about 5 minutes.

PULLED PORK BBQ
Servings: 12 | Prep: 15m | Cooks: 12h | Total: 12h15m

NUTRITION FACTS

Calories: 344 | Carbohydrates: 33.7g | Fat: 14.9g | Protein: 17.2g | Cholesterol: 52mg

INGREDIENTS

- 3 tablespoons dry barbeque rub, or more as needed
- 3/4 cup barbeque sauce, or as needed
- 1 (3 1/2) pound bone-in pork shoulder blade roast
- salt and freshly ground black pepper to taste
- 1/2 teaspoon liquid smoke flavoring, divided
- 12 soft white hamburger buns
- 1 cup water, divided
- 3/4 cup barbeque sauce, divided

DIRECTIONS

1. Preheat oven to 210 degrees F (100 degrees C).
2. Sprinkle dry rub generously on all sides of pork roast and place meat into a heavy pan or Dutch oven.
3. Pour 1/4 teaspoon of liquid smoke flavoring into each of two 6-ounce ramekins; fill ramekins with 1/2 cup water each. Place ramekins into the Dutch oven on either side of the roast. Place lid onto Dutch oven.
4. Roast pork in the preheated oven until very tender, 12 hours. Remove roast from Dutch oven, place onto a work surface (such as a cutting board), and separate the meat from the bone using your fingers. Discard any large pieces of fat.
5. Roughly chop pork with a large knife or cleaver; drizzle with 3/4 cup barbeque sauce. Season with salt and black pepper.
6. Spread about 1 tablespoon barbeque sauce onto each bun and pile pork on buns to serve.

HOT BUFFALO CHICKEN, BACON, AND CHEESE SANDWICH

Servings: 8 | Prep: 10m | Cooks: 30m | Total: 40m

NUTRITION FACTS

Calories: 566 | Carbohydrates: 44.3g | Fat: 0g | Protein: 27.9g | Cholesterol: 77.3mg

INGREDIENTS

- 6 slices bacon
- 1 loaf Italian bread, cut in half lengthwise
- 1/2 cup mayonnaise
- 3 cups shredded meat from a rotisserie chicken
- 1/4 cup sour cream
- 8 slices pepperjack cheese
- 2 tablespoons hot buffalo wing sauce
- 1/4 cup roasted red bell peppers, drained and sliced

DIRECTIONS

1. Preheat an oven to 325 degrees F (165 degrees C).
2. Place the bacon in a large, deep skillet; cook over medium-high heat, turning occasionally, until evenly browned. Drain the bacon slices on a paper towel-lined plate.
3. Combine the mayonnaise, sour cream, and hot sauce in a small bowl. Spread both halves of the bread with the mayonnaise mixture. Place chicken on bottom half of bread; layer bacon and cheese on top of chicken. Fold the top half of the bread over the bottom, and wrap with foil.
4. Bake for 20 to 25 minutes. Add a layer of red pepper slices on top of the bacon and cheese, if desired. Cut into slices, and serve.

OPEN-FACED BROILED ROAST BEEF SANDWICH

Servings: 4 | Prep: 15m | Cooks: 5m | Total: 20m

NUTRITION FACTS

Calories: 397 | Carbohydrates: 23g | Fat: g | Protein: 34.4g | Cholesterol: 77mg

INGREDIENTS

- 2 hoagie buns, split
- 2 tomatoes, thinly sliced
- 2 tablespoons mayonnaise
- 1/2 red onion, thinly sliced
- 2 teaspoons prepared coarse-ground mustard

- 4 slices provolone cheese
- 1 pound deli sliced roast beef
- salt and pepper to taste

DIRECTIONS

1. Preheat oven on broiler setting.
2. Cut rolls in half, and toast in a bread toaster. Place on a baking sheet. Spread each half with mayonnaise and mustard. Layer with roast beef, tomato, red onion, Provolone, salt and pepper.
3. Broil 3 to 6 inches from heat source for 2 to 4 minutes (keep a constant eye on it) until cheese is bubbly and is beginning to brown.

CUCUMBER SANDWICHES
Servings: 15 | Prep: 15m | Cooks: 0m | Total: 15m

NUTRITION FACTS

Calories: 48 | Carbohydrates: 1.9g | Fat: 4.3g | Protein: 0.8g | Cholesterol: 14mg

INGREDIENTS

- 1 (8 ounce) package whipped cream cheese
- 1 (.7 ounce) package dry Italian-style salad dressing mix
- 1 (1 pound) loaf cocktail rye bread
- 1 cucumber, thinly sliced

DIRECTIONS

1. In a small bowl, mix whipped cream cheese and dry Italian-style dressing mix. Spread equal portions of the mixture on slices of the cocktail rye bread. Top each with a slice of cucumber.

CHICKEN CREOLE WITH CHILE CREAM SAUCE
Servings: 4 | Prep: 20m | Cooks: 0m | Total: 20m

NUTRITION FACTS

Calories: 365.7 | Carbohydrates: 31.1g | Fat: 0g | Protein: 27.7g | Cholesterol: 73.3mg

INGREDIENTS

- 4 skinless, boneless chicken breasts
- 1 (4 ounce) can chopped green chilies
- 2 teaspoons Creole or Cajun seasoning
- 1 teaspoon lime juice

- 1 tablespoon olive oil
- 1/4 cup sour cream
- 1 (10.75 ounce) can Campbell's Condensed Cream of Chicken Soup (Regular or 98% Fat Free)
- 2 cups Hot cooked regular long-grain white rice
- 1/2 cup water

DIRECTIONS

1. Season chicken with Creole seasoning.
2. Heat oil in skillet. Add chicken and cook until browned.
3. Add soup, water, chiles and lime juice. Heat to a boil. Cook over low heat 5 minutes or until done.
4. Stir in sour cream and heat through. Serve over rice.

GRILLED CHICKEN PINEAPPLE SLIDERS
Servings: 6 | Prep: 1h | Cooks: 15m | Total: 1h15m

NUTRITION FACTS

Calories: 396.8 | Carbohydrates: 58.2g | Fat: 0g | Protein: 27.3g | Cholesterol: 73.6mg

INGREDIENTS

- 1 lemon, juiced
- 6 rings pineapple rings
- 1 lime, juiced
- 2 tablespoons teriyaki sauce
- 1 tablespoon cider vinegar
- 6 slices red onion
- 1 pinch salt and black pepper to taste
- 6 Hawaiian bread rolls - split and toasted
- 3 skinless, boneless chicken breast halves - cut in half
- 6 lettuce leaves - rinsed and dried

DIRECTIONS

1. Whisk together the lemon juice, lime juice, cider vinegar, salt and pepper in a large glass or ceramic bowl. Add the chicken and toss to evenly coat. Cover the bowl with plastic wrap, and marinate in the refrigerator for 1 hour.
2. Preheat an outdoor grill for medium-high heat, and lightly oil the grate.
3. Remove the chicken from the marinade, and shake off excess. Discard the remaining marinade. Grill the chicken for 5 to 7 minutes each side, or until juices run clear when chicken is pierced with a fork. Grill pineapple for 2 to 3 minutes per side, or until heated through and grill marks appear.

4. Spread 1 teaspoon teriyaki sauce on the bottom half of a toasted roll; next add a lettuce leaf, a piece of chicken, a pineapple round, and an onion slice. Replace the top and repeat with the remaining rolls.

SLOPPY JOES

Servings: 6 | Prep: 10m | Cooks: 1h | Total: 1h10m

NUTRITION FACTS

Calories: 229 | Carbohydrates: 4.8g | Fat: 16.3g | Protein: 14.7g | Cholesterol: 58mg

INGREDIENTS

- 1 pound lean ground beef
- 1 1/4 cups water
- 1 (10.75 ounce) can condensed chicken gumbo soup
- salt to taste
- 2 tablespoons ketchup
- ground black pepper to taste
- 1 tablespoon yellow mustard

DIRECTIONS

1. In large skillet over medium heat, brown meat. Drain any grease from pan.
2. Stir in soup, ketchup, yellow mustard, water, salt and pepper. Turn heat to medium-low; simmer uncovered for about 1 hour until liquid is absorbed and mixture is thickened.

MEATBALL GRINDERS WITH A YUMMY SAUCE

Servings: 6 | Prep: 5m | Cooks: 20m | Total: 25m

NUTRITION FACTS

Calories: 699 | Carbohydrates: 87.4g | Fat: 27.6g | Protein: 25.4g | Cholesterol: 70mg

INGREDIENTS

- 3 (14 ounce) cans pizza sauce
- 1 teaspoon freshly ground black pepper
- 1 (10 ounce) jar apple jelly
- 1 (16 ounce) package frozen meatballs
- 1 teaspoon Italian seasoning
- 6 hoagie rolls, split lengthwise
- 1 teaspoon salt

- 1 cup shredded mozzarella cheese

DIRECTIONS

1. In a large saucepan, mix pizza sauce, apple jelly, Italian seasoning, salt and pepper. Bring to a low boil over medium heat.
2. Place frozen meatballs into the sauce mixture. Cover and simmer over medium heat for 20 minutes, or until meatballs are done, stirring occasionally.
3. While the meatballs are cooking, preheat oven to 375 degrees F (190 degrees C). Place the split hoagie rolls on a large baking sheet.
4. Place several meatballs and desired amount of sauce in each roll. Layer with mozzarella cheese. Place in the preheated oven for 2 to 3 minutes, or until cheese is melted.

PANZANELLA PANINI
Servings: 1 | Prep: 10m | Cooks: 5m | Total: 15m

NUTRITION FACTS

Calories: 402 | Carbohydrates: 29.9g | Fat: 24.1g | Protein: 18.5g | Cholesterol: 36mg

INGREDIENTS

- 1 French deli roll, split
- 1 small tomato, sliced
- 1 teaspoon balsamic vinegar
- 4 fresh basil leaves
- 2 slices mozzarella cheese
- olive oil

DIRECTIONS

1. Preheat a skillet over medium-low heat.
2. Sprinkle cut sides of roll with balsamic vinegar. Layer one slice of mozzarella cheese, tomato slices, basil leaves, and the remaining slice of mozzarella cheese on the roll. Close sandwich; rub outside with olive oil.
3. Place sandwich in preheated skillet; top with another heavy skillet to press. Cook until bread is toasted and golden, about 3 minutes. Flip sandwich; top with skillet. Cook second side until toasted, about an additional 2 minutes.

DRIP BEEF SANDWICHES
Servings: 5 | Prep: 20m | Cooks: 7h | Total: 7h20m

NUTRITION FACTS

Calories: 934 | Carbohydrates: 2.5g | Fat: 61.1g | Protein: 87.9g | Cholesterol: 295mg

INGREDIENTS

- 5 pounds chuck roast
- 2 bay leaves
- 2 cubes beef bouillon
- 2 tablespoons whole black peppercorns
- 2 tablespoons salt
- 2 teaspoons dried oregano
- 2 teaspoons garlic salt
- 1 1/2 teaspoons dried rosemary

DIRECTIONS

1. Place roast in a large pot with water to cover. Mix in bouillon, salt, and garlic salt. Place the bay leaves, peppercorns, oregano, and rosemary in a coffee filter and secure tightly with a rubber band. Add this to the pot.
2. Bring to a boil over high heat, then reduce heat to low, cover with a lid, and simmer for 6 to 8 hours. Remove coffee filter and discard. Remove roast from the pot and shred with two forks. Reserve broth for dipping if desired.

JOANNE'S SUPER HERO SANDWICH

Servings: 6 | Prep: 20m | Cooks: 8h | Total: 8h20m | Additional: 8h

NUTRITION FACTS

Calories: 683 | Carbohydrates: 46.1g | Fat: 40.2g | Protein: 34.3g | Cholesterol: 92mg

INGREDIENTS

- 1/2 cup olive oil
- 1 cup mushrooms, chopped
- 1 tablespoon lemon juice
- 1 (1 pound) loaf round, crusty Italian bread
- 3 tablespoons tarragon vinegar
- 1/2 pound sliced deli turkey meat
- 3 cloves garlic, minced
- 1/2 pound sliced ham
- 2 tablespoons chopped fresh parsley
- 1/4 pound sliced salami
- 2 teaspoons dried oregano
- 1/2 pound sliced mozzarella cheese

- 1/2 teaspoon black pepper
- 6 leaves lettuce
- 1 cup black olives, chopped
- 1 tomato, sliced

DIRECTIONS

1. In a medium bowl, combine olive oil, lemon juice, vinegar and garlic. Season with parsley, oregano and pepper. stir in olives and mushrooms. Set aside.
2. Cut the off top half of the bread. Scoop out the inside, and leave a 1/2 inch outside wall. Spoon 2/3 of the olive mixture into the bottom. Layer with turkey, ham, salami, mozzarella, lettuce and tomato. Pour remaining olive mixture on top, and replace the top half of bread. Wrap securely in plastic wrap, and refrigerate overnight.

HODIE'S SLOPPY JOES
Servings: 6 | Prep: 10m | Cooks: 25m | Total: 35m

NUTRITION FACTS

Calories: 280 | Carbohydrates: 11.1g | Fat: 20.2g | Protein: 13.5g | Cholesterol: 64mg

INGREDIENTS

- 1 pound ground beef
- 1/3 cup ketchup
- 1/2 cup chopped onion
- 2 tablespoons brown sugar
- 1 (8 ounce) can tomato sauce
- 1 tablespoon apple cider vinegar

DIRECTIONS

1. Place the ground beef and chopped onion in a skillet over medium heat; cook and stir until the beef is completely browned and the onions are translucent. Drain the fat from the skillet and return it to medium heat. Stir in the tomato sauce, ketchup, brown sugar, and vinegar. Reduce heat to medium low and simmer 20 minutes.

CABBAGE BURGERS
Servings: 18 | Prep: 1m | Cooks: 20m | Total: 21m

NUTRITION FACTS

Calories: 468 | Carbohydrates: 41.2g | Fat: 19.2g | Protein: 29.7g | Cholesterol: 80mg

INGREDIENTS

- 3 (1 pound) loaves frozen bread dough, thawed
- 1 large onion, chopped
- 5 pounds ground beef
- 2 cloves garlic, chopped
- 1/4 cup water
- salt and freshly ground black pepper to taste
- 1 large head cabbage, chopped
- 2 tablespoons butter, melted

DIRECTIONS

1. Preheat the oven to 375 degrees F (190 degrees C). Divide each loaf of frozen bread dough into 6 pieces, and roll into balls. Set aside.
2. Crumble the ground beef into a large pot over medium heat. Cook and stir until evenly browned. Drain off grease. Add the water, cabbage, onion, and garlic. Cook over medium-low heat, stirring as needed, until the cabbage is soft. Season with salt and pepper to taste. I like to use more pepper than salt. Drain off any excess liquids, and set aside.
3. On a lightly floured surface, roll the dough balls into 5 inch (approximate) squares. Place about 3/4 cup of the cabbage burger into the center, fold the dough over, and pinch to seal. Place on a baking sheet with the seam side down.
4. Bake for 15 to 18 minutes in the preheated oven, or until golden brown. Remove from the oven, and brush with melted butter. Serve hot.

TURKEY WRAPS

Servings: 6 | Prep: 20m | Cooks: 0m | Total: 20m

NUTRITION FACTS

Calories: 457 | Carbohydrates: 37.1g | Fat: 28g | Protein: 24.2g | Cholesterol: 78mg

INGREDIENTS

- 1 (8 ounce) package cream cheese with chives
- 3/4 cup shredded Swiss cheese
- 2 tablespoons Dijon mustard
- 1 large tomato, seeded and diced
- 6 (8 inch) whole wheat tortillas
- 1 large avocado, sliced
- 1 1/2 cups finely shredded iceberg lettuce
- 6 slices bacon, cooked and crumbled
- 12 slices thinly sliced deli turkey

DIRECTIONS

1. Mix together the cream cheese and Dijon mustard until smooth. Spread each tortilla with about 2 tablespoons of the cream cheese mixture, spreading to within 1/4 inch of the edge of the tortillas.
2. Arrange about 1/4 cup of shredded lettuce on each tortilla, and press the lettuce down into the cream cheese mixture. Place 2 turkey slices per tortilla over the lettuce, and sprinkle with 2 tablespoons of shredded Swiss cheese. Top each tortilla evenly with tomato, avocado slices, and crumbled bacon.
3. Roll each tortilla up tightly, and cut in half across the middle with a slightly diagonal cut.

GRILLED PORTOBELLO WITH BASIL MAYONNAISE SANDWICH

Servings: 6 | Prep: 10m | Cooks: 10m | Total: 25m

NUTRITION FACTS

Calories: 412 | Carbohydrates: 35.6g | Fat: 27.7g | Protein: 8.3g | Cholesterol: 12mg

INGREDIENTS

- 1/3 cup balsamic vinegar
- 1 teaspoon lemon juice
- 1/4 cup olive oil
- 2 tablespoons chopped fresh basil
- 1 tablespoon minced garlic
- 6 kaiser rolls, split, toasted
- 6 portobello mushroom caps
- 1 tablespoon butter
- 1/2 cup mayonnaise
- 6 leaves lettuce
- 1 tablespoon Dijon mustard
- 6 tomato slices

DIRECTIONS

1. Preheat an outdoor grill for medium heat, and lightly oil the grate. Whisk together the balsamic vinegar, olive oil, and garlic in a small bowl.
2. Arrange the portobello mushrooms gill-side up on a tray or baking sheet. Brush the mushrooms with some of the vinegar mixture, and allow to marinate for 3 to 5 minutes.
3. Place the marinated mushrooms on the preheated grill, gill-side down. Grill mushrooms until tender, brushing both sides of the mushrooms with the remaining marinade, about 4 minutes on each side.
4. Mix the mayonnaise, dijon mustard, lemon juice, and basil in a small bowl. Butter the toasted kaiser rolls, then spread with the mayonnaise mixture. Divide the mushrooms, lettuce, and tomato slices evenly to make 6 sandwiches.

SLOW COOKER GROUND BEEF BARBECUE

Servings: 20 | Prep: 10m | Cooks: 6h15m | Total: 6h25m

NUTRITION FACTS

Calories: 188 | Carbohydrates: 14.5g | Fat: 8.5g | Protein: 13.9g | Cholesterol: 45mg

INGREDIENTS

- 3 pounds lean ground beef
- 1/2 teaspoon ground black pepper
- 1 large onion, chopped
- 1 tablespoon cider vinegar
- 2 cloves garlic, minced
- 2 tablespoons prepared mustard
- 5 stalks celery, finely chopped
- 1/4 cup firmly packed brown sugar
- 1 1/2 teaspoons salt
- 3 1/2 cups ketchup

DIRECTIONS

1. Place ground beef in a large skillet over medium heat, and cook until brown, breaking up the meat as it cooks, about 15 minutes. Drain excess grease.
2. Place the cooked meat, onion, garlic, celery, salt, black pepper, cider vinegar, mustard, brown sugar, and ketchup into a slow cooker, and stir to combine. Set the cooker on Low, and cook for 6 to 8 hours.

TUNA PITA MELTS

Servings: 6 | Prep: 10m | Cooks: 10m | Total: 20m

NUTRITION FACTS

Calories: 346 | Carbohydrates: 35.2g | Fat: 12.4g | Protein: 22.2g | Cholesterol: 38mg

INGREDIENTS

- 6 (6-inch) pitas
- 1/2 teaspoon dried dill
- 2 (5 ounce) cans tuna, drained
- 1/4 teaspoon salt
- 2 tablespoons mayonnaise
- 1 large tomato, sliced into thin wedges
- 2 tablespoons dill pickle relish

- 1 cup shredded Cheddar cheese

DIRECTIONS

1. Preheat the oven to 400 degrees F (200 degrees C). Place the whole pita breads in a single layer on a baking sheet. Bake for 5 minutes, or until lightly toasted.
2. In a medium bowl, mix together the tuna, mayonnaise, relish, dill and salt. Spread an equal amount of the tuna mixture onto each of the pita breads. Arrange tomato wedges over the tuna, and sprinkle with shredded Cheddar cheese.
3. Bake for 5 minutes in the preheated oven, or until cheese has melted.

BACHELOR GRILLED CHEESE
Servings: 1 | Prep: 2m | Cooks: 0m | Total: 2m

NUTRITION FACTS

Calories: 346 | Carbohydrates: 26.2g | Fat: 19.4g | Protein: 16.4g | Cholesterol: 53mg

INGREDIENTS

- 2 slices white bread
- 2 slices American cheese

DIRECTIONS

1. Toast bread in a toaster until golden. Place slices of cheese between the two pieces of toast. Wrap sandwich in a paper towel, and heat in the microwave for 15 to 20 seconds, or until cheese is melted.

TERRI'S SLOPPY JOES
Servings: 6 | Prep: 5m | Cooks: 30m | Total: 35m

NUTRITION FACTS

Calories: 260 | Carbohydrates: 14.6g | Fat: 13.5g | Protein: 19.8g | Cholesterol: 69mg

INGREDIENTS

- 1 1/2 pounds ground beef
- 1 tablespoon vinegar
- 1 small onion, chopped
- 1 tablespoon prepared mustard
- 3/4 cup ketchup
- 1 tablespoon white sugar
- 1/4 cup barbeque sauce

DIRECTIONS

1. Cook and stir the ground beef and onion in a large skillet over medium heat until the beef is completely browned and the onion softens, about 10 minutes.
2. Stir the ketchup, barbeque sauce, vinegar, mustard, and white sugar through the ground beef mixture; simmer 15 minutes.

TOFU SANDWICH SPREAD
Servings: 4 | Prep: 15m | Cooks: 0m | Total: 15m

NUTRITION FACTS

Calories: 370.2 | Carbohydrates: 7.2g | Fat: 0g | Protein: 18.8g | Cholesterol: 10.4mg

INGREDIENTS

- 1 pound firm tofu
- 1/2 cup mayonnaise
- 1 stalk celery, chopped
- 2 tablespoons soy sauce
- 1 green onion, chopped
- 1 tablespoon lemon juice

DIRECTIONS

1. Drain the block of tofu, and freeze overnight. Thaw, and cut into quarters. Squeeze out any moisture by hand, then wrap in paper towels, and squeeze again. Crumble into a medium bowl.
2. Add celery and green onion to the tofu. Stir in mayonnaise, soy sauce and lemon juice until well blended.

JEREMY'S PHILLY STEAK AND CHEESE SANDWICH
Servings: 4 | Prep: 15m | Cooks: 15m | Total: 30m

NUTRITION FACTS

Calories: 654 | Carbohydrates: 70.2g | Fat: 28.6g | Protein: 29.9g | Cholesterol: 91mg

INGREDIENTS

- 1 teaspoon butter
- 3/4 cup cream cheese, softened
- 1/2 white onion, sliced
- 1 teaspoon Worcestershire sauce
- 1/2 red onion, sliced

- salt and pepper to taste
- 8 fresh mushrooms, sliced
- 1 French baguette, cut in half lengthwise
- 1 clove garlic, minced
- 1/2 cup shredded Swiss cheese
- 6 ounces beef sirloin, thinly sliced

DIRECTIONS

1. Melt butter in a large skillet over medium-high heat. Saute the white and red onions, mushrooms, and garlic until tender. Remove from the pan, and set aside.
2. Place the sliced beef in the pan, and fry until no longer pink, about 5 minutes. Reduce heat to low, and stir in the cream cheese and Worcestershire sauce, cooking and stirring until the beef is well coated. Season with salt and pepper to taste.
3. Meanwhile, preheat your oven's broiler.
4. Place beef mixture onto bottom half of the baguette, then cover the beef with the onion mixture. Place Swiss cheese over the onion mixture. Place open sandwich under a hot broiler until the cheese is melted. Place top of baguette onto the toppings, and serve.

DAN'S FAVORITE CHICKEN SANDWICH
Servings: 2 | Prep: 15m | Cooks: 35m | Total: 50m

NUTRITION FACTS

Calories: 1062.7 | Carbohydrates: 84.8g | Fat: 0g | Protein: 59.8g | Cholesterol: 143.2mg

INGREDIENTS

- 2 skinless, boneless chicken breast halves
- 2 tablespoons Ranch dressing
- 2 tablespoons barbeque sauce
- 4 slices Swiss cheese
- 4 slices bacon
- 1 small avocado - peeled, pitted and diced
- 2 eaches hoagie rolls, split lengthwise

DIRECTIONS

1. Preheat oven to 375 degrees F (190 degrees C). Coat a baking dish with cooking spray. Brush both sides of each chicken breast with barbeque sauce and place in the baking dish. Top each breast with 2 slices bacon.
2. Bake chicken 25 minutes in the preheated oven, until juices run clear. Drain bacon strips on paper towels, and slice breasts in half lengthwise.

3. Heat the oven broiler. Spread both halves of each hoagie roll with Ranch dressing. Place 2 breast halves on one half of each roll. Place 2 strips of bacon on each remaining roll half. Top each half with 1 slice Swiss cheese.
4. Arrange sandwich halves on the baking sheet, and broil 2 to 5 minutes, until the cheese is melted and bubbly. Layer chicken halves of sandwiches with avocado slices, and top with bacon halves to serve.

LORRAINE'S CLUB SANDWICH
Servings: 1 | Prep: 5m | Cooks: 5m | Total: 10m

NUTRITION FACTS

Calories: 818 | Carbohydrates: 44.2g | Fat: 61.7g | Protein: 22.4g | Cholesterol: 76mg

INGREDIENTS

- 2 slices bacon
- 2 leaves lettuce
- 3 slices bread, toasted
- 2 (1 ounce) slices cooked deli turkey breast
- 3 tablespoons mayonnaise
- 2 slices tomato

DIRECTIONS

1. Place bacon in a heavy skillet. Cook over medium high heat until evenly brown. Drain on paper towels.
2. Spread each slice of bread with mayonnaise. On one slice of toast, place the turkey and lettuce. Cover with a slice of toast, then the bacon and tomato. Top with last slice of toast.

SLOW COOKER PHILLY STEAK SANDWICH MEAT
Servings: 4 | Prep: 15m | Cooks: 8m | Total: 8h23m | Additional: 8h

NUTRITION FACTS

Calories: 251 | Carbohydrates: 60g | Fat: 10.6g | Protein: 20.1g | Cholesterol: 60mg

INGREDIENTS

- 1/2 large onion, sliced
- 1/4 teaspoon dried marjoram
- 3 cloves garlic, chopped
- 1/4 teaspoon dried basil
- 1 pound beef sirloin, cut into 2-inch strips, or more to taste
- 2 tablespoons bourbon whiskey (such as Jim Beam)

- 1/2 teaspoon ground cumin
- 1 teaspoon soy sauce
- 1/2 teaspoon ground black pepper
- 1 teaspoon prepared mustard
- 1/2 teaspoon chili powder
- 1 teaspoon Worcestershire sauce
- 1/2 teaspoon onion powder
- 1/2 teaspoon hot sauce (such as Frank's Red Hot)
- 1/2 teaspoon garlic powder
- 1 (12 fluid ounce) can or bottle beer (such as Budweiser)
- 1/4 teaspoon paprika
- 2 cubes beef bouillon
- 1/4 teaspoon dried thyme

DIRECTIONS

1. Spread onion and garlic into the bottom of a slow cooker; layer beef over onion and garlic. Sprinkle cumin, black pepper, chili powder, onion powder, garlic powder, paprika, thyme, marjoram, and basil over beef; top with bourbon, soy sauce, mustard, Worcestershire sauce, and hot sauce. Pour beer over beef mixture and add beef bouillon cubes.
2. Cook on Low, stirring every hour or so, for 8 hours (or High for 4 hours).

CHICKEN SALAD WRAPS
Servings: 6 | Prep: 10m | Cooks: 0m | Total: 10m

NUTRITION FACTS

Calories: 463.7 | Carbohydrates: 42.5g | Fat: 0g | Protein: 27.2g | Cholesterol: 61.4mg

INGREDIENTS

- 2 (10 ounce) cans chunk chicken, drained and flaked
- salt and pepper to taste
- 1/4 cup chopped onion
- 6 (10 inch) flour tortillas
- 1/4 cup mayonnaise
- 12 lettuce leaves
- 4 tablespoons fresh salsa

DIRECTIONS

1. In a small bowl combine the chicken, onion, mayonnaise, salsa, salt and pepper. Mix together.
2. Line each tortilla with two lettuce leaves, then divide chicken salad mixture evenly among each tortilla and roll up, or 'wrap'.

GRILLED GYRO BURGERS
Servings: 6 | Prep: 30m | Cooks: 14m | Total: 44m

NUTRITION FACTS

Calories: 590 | Carbohydrates: 44.3g | Fat: 32.1g | Protein: 28.9g | Cholesterol: 101mg

INGREDIENTS

- 2 (8 ounce) containers plain yogurt, divided
- 1/4 cup diced onion
- 1 (1 ounce) package dry Ranch-style dressing mix
- 6 pita bread rounds
- 1 cucumber, peeled, seeded, and chopped
- 2 cups torn lettuce leaves
- 1 1/2 pounds ground beef
- 1 tomato, seeded and diced

DIRECTIONS

1. In a medium bowl, combine 1 container of plain yogurt with the envelope of ranch dressing mix. Remove half of the mixture to another bowl. Into one of the bowls, add the remaining container of plain yogurt and diced cucumber; mix well. Cover and refrigerate. Preheat grill and lightly oil grate.
2. Mix the ground beef and 1/4 cup onion into the remaining half of the yogurt mixture. Shape into 6 hamburger patties.
3. Grill patties on medium heat for 7 minutes each side, turning once.
4. Cut off 1/4 end of the pita pockets and fill with torn lettuce, grilled burger, creamy cucumber sauce and diced tomatoes.

HOT HAM AND CHEESE SANDWICHES
Servings: 8 | Prep: 10m | Cooks: 20m | Total: 30m

NUTRITION FACTS

Calories: 360 | Carbohydrates: 23.8g | Fat: 21.7g | Protein: 17.4g | Cholesterol: 58mg

INGREDIENTS

- 1/4 cup butter, softened
- 1 teaspoon dill seed
- 2 tablespoons prepared horseradish mustard
- 8 slices Swiss cheese
- 2 tablespoons chopped onions
- 8 slices cooked ham

- 1 teaspoon poppy seeds
- 8 hamburger buns

DIRECTIONS

1. Preheat oven to 250 degrees F (120 degrees C).
2. Combine butter, mustard, onions, poppy seeds and dill seed. Spread insides of buns with this mixture. Place a slice of cheese and a slice of ham inside each bun.
3. Wrap buns in foil and place in preheated oven. Bake for 15 to 20 minutes, until cheese has melted.

CURRIED CHICKEN TEA SANDWICHES
Servings: 6 | Prep: 20m | Cooks: 0m | Total: 20m

NUTRITION FACTS

Calories: 528.5 | Carbohydrates: 43.9g | Fat: 0g | Protein: 16.5g | Cholesterol: 46.9mg

INGREDIENTS

- 2 cups cubed, cooked chicken
- 3/4 cup mayonnaise
- 1 unpeeled red apple, chopped
- 2 teaspoons lime juice
- 3/4 cup dried cranberries
- 1/2 teaspoon curry powder
- 1/2 cup thinly sliced celery
- 12 slices bread
- 1/4 cup chopped pecans
- 12 lettuce leaves
- 2 tablespoons thinly sliced green onions

DIRECTIONS

1. Combine chicken, apple, cranberries, celery, pecans, and green onions in a bowl. Mix mayonnaise, lime juice, and curry powder in a small bowl. Fold mayonnaise mixture into chicken mixture; stir to coat. Cover and refrigerate until ready to serve.
2. Cut each bread slice with a 3-inch heart-shaped cookie cutter; top with a lettuce leaf and chicken salad.

GRIDDLE STYLE PHILLY STEAK SANDWICHES
Servings: 4 | Prep: 5m | Cooks: 15m | Total: 20m

NUTRITION FACTS

Calories: 741 | Carbohydrates: 76.6g | Fat: 25.7g | Protein: 50.4g | Cholesterol: 94mg

INGREDIENTS

- 1 (8 ounce) can sliced mushrooms, drained
- salt to taste
- 1 small onion, sliced
- seasoned salt to taste
- 1 green bell pepper, seeded and sliced into strips
- 1 pound thinly sliced roast beef
- 8 slices provolone cheese
- 4 submarine rolls, halved

DIRECTIONS

1. Preheat an electric griddle or stovetop griddle over medium-high heat. On one half of the griddle, place the mushrooms, onion and pepper. On the other side, place the roast beef. Cook and stir each group separately, chopping the beef into smaller pieces as it cooks, and seasoning with salt and seasoned salt.
2. When the vegetables are tender and the beef is hot, place the slices of provolone cheese over the beef to melt. Turn off the griddle. Scoop the cheesy grilled beef into sandwich rolls, and top with the onions and peppers.

SUPER EASY SLOPPY JOES

Servings: 6 | Prep: 10m | Cooks: 20m | Total: 30m

NUTRITION FACTS

Calories: 536 | Carbohydrates: 13.7g | Fat: 35.4g | Protein: 38.1g | Cholesterol: 139mg

INGREDIENTS

- 3 pounds ground beef
- 1/4 cup apple cider vinegar
- 1 cup chopped yellow onion
- 1/4 cup packed brown sugar
- 1 cup finely chopped celery
- 1 teaspoon prepared yellow mustard (optional)
- 1 (12 ounce) bottle tomato-based chili sauce

DIRECTIONS

1. Crumble the ground beef into a large pot or Dutch oven over medium-high heat. Cook, stirring frequently until evenly browned. Drain off grease. Add the onion and celery, and cook until the onion is tender, about 3 minutes.
2. Reduce heat to medium and pour in the chili sauce. Stir in the vinegar and sugar. Add mustard if using. Simmer until the mixture is your desired thickness. Serve on buns.

CARRIE'S GARLIC PESTO TUNA SALAD SANDWICHES
Servings: 4 | Prep: 10m | Cooks: 0m | Total: 10m

NUTRITION FACTS

Calories: 342 | Carbohydrates: 34.6g | Fat: 11.9g | Protein: 23.8g | Cholesterol: 24mg

INGREDIENTS

- 2 (5 ounce) cans tuna in water, drained
- 2 cloves garlic, minced
- 2 tablespoons mayonnaise
- 8 slices rye bread
- 1 tablespoon prepared mustard
- 8 leaves lettuce
- 2 tablespoons basil pesto
- 1 large ripe tomato, sliced

DIRECTIONS

1. In a medium bowl, mix together tuna, mayonnaise, mustard, pesto, and garlic.
2. Make four sandwiches by layering tuna, lettuce, and tomato slices between slices of bread. Serve.

BUFFALO CHICKEN AND RANCH WRAPS
Servings: 12 | Prep: 20 | Cooks: 45m | Total: 1h5m

NUTRITION FACTS

Calories: 526.5 | Carbohydrates: 38.6g | Fat: 0g | Protein: 36.4g | Cholesterol: 92mg

INGREDIENTS

- 1 pound thin-sliced bacon
- 2 tablespoons butter, melted
- 2 tablespoons bacon drippings
- 12 (10 inch) flour tortillas
- 3 pounds skinless, boneless chicken breast halves, cut into bite size pieces

- 1 cup diced fresh tomato
- 1/4 cup Buffalo wing sauce
- 3/4 cup ranch dressing, divided

DIRECTIONS

1. Place the bacon in a large, deep skillet, and cook over medium-high heat, turning occasionally, until evenly browned and crisp, 10 to 15 minutes. Drain the bacon slices on a paper towel-lined plate. Crumble when cool.
2. Drain off all but 2 tablespoons of the bacon drippings, and cook and stir the chicken breast chunks until browned, about 10 minutes. Cover the skillet and allow chicken to continue cooking until no longer pink inside and the juices run clear, about 10 more minutes. Stir in the Buffalo sauce and melted butter until chicken is thoroughly coated. Stir in the crumbled bacon. Keep the mixture warm.
3. Heat the tortillas, one at a time, in a large ungreased skillet over medium heat until they begin to form air bubbles and small brown spots. Fill each each warmed tortilla with about 1/3 cup of the chicken filling and a tablespoon or so of tomatoes; sprinkle the tomatoes with 1 tablespoon of ranch dressing. Wrap the tortilla around the filling; serve warm.

CAMPBELL'S SLOW-COOKED PULLED PORK SANDWICHES

Servings: 12 | Prep: 15m | Cooks: 8h10m | Total: 8h25m

NUTRITION FACTS

Calories: 344 | Carbohydrates: 31.2g | Fat: 16.1g | Protein: 17.9g | Cholesterol: 53mg

INGREDIENTS

- 1 tablespoon vegetable oil
- 1/4 cup cider vinegar
- 3 1/2 pounds boneless pork shoulder roast, netted or tied
- 3 tablespoons packed brown sugar
- 1 (10.5 ounce) can Campbell's Condensed French Onion Soup
- 12 round sandwich rolls or hamburger rolls, split
- 1 cup ketchup

DIRECTIONS

1. Heat the oil in a 10-inch skillet over medium-high heat. Add the pork and cook until it's well browned on all sides.
2. Stir the soup, ketchup, vinegar and brown sugar in a 5-quart slow cooker. Add the pork and turn to coat.
3. Cover and cook on LOW for 8 to 9 hours* or until the pork is fork-tender.
4. Remove the pork from the cooker to a cutting board and let stand for 10 minutes. Using 2 forks, shred the pork. Return the pork to the cooker.

5. Divide the pork and sauce mixture among the rolls.

VEGETARIAN SLOPPY JOES

Servings: 6 | Prep: 20m | Cooks: 20m | Total: 40m

NUTRITION FACTS

Calories: 384 | Carbohydrates: 37.3g | Fat: 19.6g | Protein: 18.3g | Cholesterol: 0mg

INGREDIENTS

- 1/4 cup vegetable oil
- 1/4 teaspoon celery seed
- 1/2 cup minced onion
- 1/4 teaspoon ground cumin
- 2 (8 ounce) packages tempeh
- 1/4 teaspoon salt
- 1/2 cup minced green bell pepper
- 1/2 teaspoon ground coriander
- 2 cloves garlic, minced
- 1/2 teaspoon dried thyme
- 1/4 cup tomato sauce
- 1/2 teaspoon oregano
- 1 tablespoon vegetarian Worcestershire sauce
- 1/2 teaspoon paprika
- 1 tablespoon honey
- 1 pinch ground black pepper
- 1 tablespoon blackstrap molasses
- hamburger buns
- 1/4 teaspoon cayenne pepper

DIRECTIONS

1. Heat oil in a deep, 10-inch skillet over medium-low heat. Cook the onion in the oil until translucent. Crumble the tempeh into the skillet; cook and stir until golden brown. Add the green pepper and garlic; cook another 2 to 3 minutes.
2. Stir in the tomato sauce, Worcestershire sauce, honey, molasses, cayenne pepper, celery seed, cumin, salt, coriander, thyme, oregano, paprika, and black pepper; stir. Simmer another 10 to 15 minutes. Spoon hot onto hamburger buns to serve.

GREEK GRILLED CHEESE

Servings: 1 | Prep: 5m | Cooks: 5m | Total: 10m

NUTRITION FACTS

Calories: 482 | Carbohydrates: 27.1g | Fat: 30.9g | Protein: 24.6g | Cholesterol: 92mg

INGREDIENTS

- 1 1/2 teaspoons butter, softened
- 2 slices Cheddar cheese
- 2 slices whole wheat bread, or your favorite bread
- 1 tablespoon chopped red onion
- 2 tablespoons crumbled feta cheese
- 1/4 tomato, thinly sliced

DIRECTIONS

1. Heat a skillet over medium heat. Butter one side of each slice of bread. On the non buttered side of one slice, layer the feta cheese, Cheddar cheese, red onion and tomato. Top with the other slice of bread with the butter side out.
2. Fry the sandwich until golden brown on each side, about 2 minutes per side. The second side always cooks faster.

SLOPPY SAMS

Servings: 4 | Prep: 15m | Cooks: 35m | Total: 50m

NUTRITION FACTS

Calories: 517 | Carbohydrates: 82.2g | Fat: 13.9g | Protein: 19.3g | Cholesterol: 0mg

INGREDIENTS

- 3 cups water
- 1/2 cup ketchup
- 1 cup lentils, rinsed
- 1 teaspoon mustard powder
- salt to taste (optional)
- 1 tablespoon chili powder
- 1 cup chopped onion
- 3 tablespoons molasses
- 3 tablespoons olive oil
- 1 dash Worcestershire sauce
- 2 cups chopped tomato
- salt and ground black pepper to taste
- 2 cloves garlic, minced
- 4 hamburger buns, split

- 1/2 (6 ounce) can tomato paste

DIRECTIONS

1. Combine water and lentils in a saucepan; season to taste with salt if desired. Bring to a boil over high heat, then reduce heat to medium-low, cover, and simmer until tender, about 30 minutes, stirring occasionally.
2. Meanwhile, cook onions with the olive oil in a large skillet over medium heat until the onions have softened and turned translucent, about 4 minutes. Add tomatoes and garlic, and cook for 5 minutes. Stir in tomato paste, ketchup, mustard powder, chili powder, molasses and Worcestershire sauce; simmer 5 to10 minutes until thickened.
3. Drain lentils and reserve cooking liquid. Stir lentils into sauce mixture, adding cooking liquid or water as needed to obtain the desired "sloppy joe" consistency. Serve on buns.

MY FAVORITE SLOPPY JOES
Servings: 6 | Prep: 10m | Cooks: 40m | Total: 50m

NUTRITION FACTS

Calories: 247 | Carbohydrates: 19.6g | Fat: 12g | Protein: 16.1g | Cholesterol: 50mg

INGREDIENTS

- 1 pound lean ground beef
- 1 tablespoon Worcestershire sauce, or more to taste
- 1 cup ketchup
- 1 tablespoon liquid smoke flavoring
- 1/4 cup dried minced onion
- 1 teaspoon minced garlic
- 3 tablespoons brown sugar, or to taste
- 1 cup beef broth
- 2 tablespoons spicy brown mustard
- salt and ground black pepper to taste

DIRECTIONS

1. Cook and stir ground beef in a skillet over medium heat until meat is browned and crumbly, about 10 minutes; drain excess grease. Mix ketchup, dried onion, brown sugar, mustard, Worcestershire sauce, smoke flavoring, and garlic into beef, stirring until brown sugar has dissolved.
2. Stir beef broth into beef mixture and bring to a boil; reduce heat to low and simmer until thick, about 30 minutes. Season with salt and black pepper.

SLOW COOKER VENISON SLOPPY JOES
Servings: 4 | Prep: 5m | Cooks: 8hm | Total: 8h5m

NUTRITION FACTS

Calories: 538 | Carbohydrates: 41.1g | Fat: 18.4g | Protein: 51.8g | Cholesterol: 191mg

INGREDIENTS

- 1/4 pound bacon
- 1 teaspoon chili powder
- 2 pounds venison stew meat
- 2 tablespoons minced garlic
- 1 large yellow onion, chopped
- 1 tablespoon prepared Dijon-style mustard
- 1/2 cup brown sugar
- 1 cup ketchup
- 1/4 cup wine vinegar
- salt and pepper to taste
- 1 tablespoon ground cumin

DIRECTIONS

1. Place bacon in a large, deep skillet. Cook over medium high heat until evenly brown. Remove from skillet, crumble and set aside. Brown stew meat in bacon grease for flavor.
2. Put onion, sugar, vinegar, cumin, chili powder, garlic, mustard, ketchup, salt and pepper in slow cooker and mix well. Add bacon and venison and stir together.
3. Cook for a minimum of 8 hours on Low setting. Use a fork to separate the meat into a thick and yummy Sloppy Joe-style barbecue.

THE REAL REUBEN
Servings: 1 | Prep: 5m | Cooks: 3m | Total: 8m

NUTRITION FACTS

Calories: 874 | Carbohydrates: 52.8g | Fat: 58.7g | Protein: 36g | Cholesterol: 152mg

INGREDIENTS

- 2 slices dark rye bread
- 2 slices Swiss cheese
- 1/4 pound thinly sliced corned beef
- 1/4 cup thousand island dressing
- 3 ounces sauerkraut, drained

DIRECTIONS

1. Place bread on baking sheet or broiling pan. Layer corned beef, sauerkraut and cheese on top of bread slices.
2. Broil on high heat for 3 to 4 minutes, until cheese has melted. Serve hot with Thousand Island dressing.

CHICKEN, FETA CHEESE, AND SUN-DRIED TOMATO WRAPS

Servings: 4 | Prep: 15m | Cooks: 30m | Total: 3h45m | Additional: 3h

NUTRITION FACTS

Calories: 323.8 | Carbohydrates: 34.1g | Fat: 0g | Protein: 20.7g | Cholesterol: 44.1mg

INGREDIENTS

- 2 (4 ounce) skinless, boneless chicken breast halves
- 1/3 cup crumbled feta cheese
- 1/4 cup sun-dried tomato dressing
- 4 cups loosely packed torn fresh spinach
- 8 sun-dried tomatoes (not oil packed)
- 4 eaches (10 inch) whole wheat tortillas
- 1 cup boiling water
- 1/4 cup sun-dried tomato dressing

DIRECTIONS

1. In a large resealable plastic bag, combine chicken breasts and 1/4 cup dressing. Seal, and refrigerate for several hours.
2. Preheat grill for high heat. Combine sun-dried tomatoes and hot water in a small bowl. Set aside for 10 minutes, drain, and cut tomatoes into thin slices.
3. Lightly oil grill grate. Discard marinade, and place chicken on grill. Cook for 12 to 15 minutes, turning once, or until done.
4. Cut chicken into strips, and place in a medium bowl with sliced tomatoes, feta, and spinach. Toss with remaining 1/4 cup dressing. Distribute mixture between the four tortillas, and wrap. Either cut in half and enjoy cold, or place briefly back on grill until the tortilla turns warm and crispy.

GRILLED TURKEY REUBEN SANDWICHES

Servings: 2 | Prep: 10m | Cooks: 10m | Total: 20m

NUTRITION FACTS

Calories: 760 | Carbohydrates: 48.9g | Fat: 43.9g | Protein: 44.7g | Cholesterol: 150mg

INGREDIENTS

- 1 cup sauerkraut, drained
- 4 slices marble rye bread
- 10 ounces sliced deli turkey meat
- 4 slices Swiss cheese
- 2 tablespoons butter
- 4 tablespoons thousand island salad dressing, or to taste

DIRECTIONS

1. Warm the sauerkraut and turkey, separately, in a microwave-safe bowls for 30-seconds; set aside. Spread butter generously on one side of each slice of rye bread, then spread the thousand island dressing on the other side. Divide the sauerkraut, turkey, and Swiss cheese on two slice of bread with the butter-side down. Stack the remaining two slices of bread with the butter-side up on top.
2. Heat a large skillet over medium-low heat. Arrange the sandwiches on the skillet and grill until lightly browned and the cheese is melted, about 3 minutes on each side.

GRILLED CHEESE DE MAYOO
Servings: 1 | Prep: 10m | Cooks: 5m | Total: 15m

NUTRITION FACTS

Calories: 500 | Carbohydrates: 27.2g | Fat: 34.9g | Protein: 19.5g | Cholesterol: 74mg

INGREDIENTS

- 1 tablespoon mayonnaise, divided
- 2 slices white bread
- 2 slices American cheese
- 1 slice pepperjack cheese

DIRECTIONS

1. Spread 1/2 the mayonnaise onto one side of a slice of bread and place, mayonnaise-side down, in a skillet. Place American cheese and pepperjack cheese on top of the bread. Spread remaining mayonnaise onto one side of the remaining bread and place, mayonnaise-side up, on top of the cheese.
2. Cook sandwich in the skillet over medium heat until cheese melts and the bread is golden brown, about 2 1/2 minutes per side.

M'S SLOPPY JOE SAUCE
Servings: 4 | Prep: 20m | Cooks: 15m | Total: 35m

NUTRITION FACTS

Calories: 287 | Carbohydrates: 21g | Fat: 12.4g | Protein: 24.6g | Cholesterol: 84mg

INGREDIENTS

- 1 tablespoon extra-virgin olive oil
- 1/4 cup barbeque sauce (such as KC Masterpiece)
- 1 large onion, diced
- 2 tablespoons ketchup
- 1 green bell pepper, diced
- 2 tablespoons white vinegar
- 1 tablespoon minced garlic
- 2 tablespoons Worcestershire sauce
- 1 pound ground turkey
- 1 tablespoon brown mustard
- 1 cup canned pureed tomatoes
- 1 tablespoon chile-garlic sauce (such as Sriracha)

DIRECTIONS

1. Heat the olive oil in a skillet over medium heat; cook the onion and bell pepper in the hot oil until they begin to soften, about 5 minutes. Add the garlic and ground turkey to the skillet; cook and stir until the turkey is completely crumbled and browned, another 5 to 7 minutes.
2. Stir the pureed tomatoes, barbeque sauce, ketchup, vinegar, Worcestershire sauce, mustard, and chile-garlic sauce into the turkey mixture. Simmer until completely heated, 7 to 10 minutes more.

DIVINE SUMMERTIME CHICKEN SANDWICH
Servings: 2 | Prep: 10m | Cooks: 20m | Total: 30m

NUTRITION FACTS

Calories: 671.2 | Carbohydrates: 49.6g | Fat: 0g | Protein: 39g | Cholesterol: 160.1mg

INGREDIENTS

- 4 ounces cream cheese, softened
- 2 skinless, boneless chicken breast halves
- 4 teaspoons dried dill weed, divided
- 1 small tomato, diced
- 4 tablespoons minced garlic, divided
- 1 leaf lettuce
- 2 tablespoons butter, softened
- 4 thick slices French bread

DIRECTIONS

1. In a medium bowl, mix together the cream cheese, 2 teaspoons of dill, and 2 tablespoons of garlic. Set aside.
2. Melt about half of the butter in a skillet over medium heat. Season chicken breast halves with remaining garlic and dill. Cook for about 8 minutes per side, or until the meat is firm and juices run clear. Remove from the pan, and set aside.
3. Spread the remaining butter onto one side of the slices of bread, and toast in the skillet until golden. Spread the cream cheese onto the other sides of the bread, and make sandwiches with the chicken breasts, lettuce, and tomato.

GRILLED ROASTED RED PEPPER AND HAM SANDWICH

Servings: 1 | Prep: 10m | Cooks: 10m | Total: 20m

NUTRITION FACTS

Calories: 551 | Carbohydrates: 32.1g | Fat: 35.1g | Protein: 27.1g | Cholesterol: 84mg

INGREDIENTS

- 2 teaspoons mayonnaise, or condiment of your choice (optional)
- 1/2 roasted red pepper packed in oil, drained and sliced
- 2 slices sourdough bread
- 2 teaspoons butter
- 2 slices provolone cheese
- 2 teaspoons grated Parmesan or Romano cheese
- 2 thin slices ham

DIRECTIONS

1. Spread mayonnaise onto one side of each slice of bread. On one slice of bread, place one slice of provolone cheese, then ham, red peppers, and the other slice of cheese. Top with the other slice of bread with the mayonnaise facing the filling. Butter the outsides of the sandwich, and sprinkle a little bit of Parmesan cheese onto the butter.
2. Heat a skillet over medium heat until warm. Fry the sandwich on both sides until golden brown and cheese is melted. If you have an indoor grill, this sandwich may be grilled that way also. Cut the sandwich in half, and serve.

IGNACIO'S SUPER PEANUT BUTTER AND JELLY SANDWICH

Servings: 1 | Prep: 10m | Cooks: 0m | Total: 10m

NUTRITION FACTS

Calories: 501 | Carbohydrates: 71.6g | Fat: 18.9g | Protein: 14g | Cholesterol: 0mg

INGREDIENTS

- 3 slices bread
- 2 tablespoons fruit preserves, any flavor
- 2 tablespoons peanut butter

DIRECTIONS

1. Toast 1 bread slice, allow to cool. Spread one side of each of the two remaining slices with preserves. Spread both sides of the toasted slice with peanut butter. Form a sandwich with the toasted slice in the center.

BAR-B-Q

Servings: 10 | Prep: 15m | Cooks: 30m | Total: 45m

NUTRITION FACTS

Calories: 480 | Carbohydrates: 41.7g | Fat: 21.5g | Protein: 29.3g | Cholesterol: 83mg

INGREDIENTS

- 3 pounds lean ground beef
- 1/2 cup ketchup
- 1 (10.75 ounce) can condensed tomato soup
- 1/2 cup packed brown sugar
- 1 (10.5 ounce) can condensed French onion soup
- 10 hamburger buns

DIRECTIONS

1. In a large skillet over medium heat, brown the ground beef; drain fat.
2. Pour in tomato and French onion soups. Fill each can a quarter full with water to rinse the cans out. Pour into meat mixture. Add ketchup and brown sugar. Mix thoroughly.
3. Let simmer for 30 minutes. Serve on hamburger buns.

TURKEY AVOCADO PANINI

Servings: 2 | Prep: 17m | Cooks: 8m | Total: 25m

NUTRITION FACTS

Calories: 723 | Carbohydrates: 42.1g | Fat: 51.3g | Protein: 25.3g | Cholesterol: 62mg

INGREDIENTS

- 1/2 ripe avocado
- 2 slices provolone cheese
- 1/4 cup mayonnaise
- 1 cup whole fresh spinach leaves, divided
- 2 ciabatta rolls
- 1/4 pound thinly sliced mesquite smoked turkey breast
- 1 tablespoon olive oil, divided
- 2 roasted red peppers, sliced into strips

DIRECTIONS

1. Mash the avocado and the mayonnaise together in a bowl until thoroughly mixed.
2. Preheat a panini sandwich press.
3. To make the sandwiches, split the ciabatta rolls in half the flat way, and brush the bottom of each roll with olive oil. Place the bottoms of the rolls onto the panini press, olive oil side down. Place a provolone cheese slice, half the spinach leaves, half the sliced turkey breast, and a sliced roasted red pepper on each sandwich. Spread half of the avocado mixture on the cut surface of each top, and place the top of the roll on the sandwich. Brush the top of the roll with olive oil.
4. Close the panini press and cook until the bun is toasted and crisp, with golden brown grill marks, and the cheese has melted, about 5 to 8 minutes.

VENISON GYROS

Servings: 6 | Prep: 15m | Cooks: 30m | Total: 2h45m

NUTRITION FACTS

Calories: 432 | Carbohydrates: 33.7g | Fat: 10.2g | Protein: 48.4g | Cholesterol: 159mg

INGREDIENTS

- 2 tablespoons olive oil
- 1 tablespoon dried oregano
- 1 1/2 tablespoons ground cumin
- 1 tablespoon red wine vinegar
- 1 tablespoon minced garlic
- salt and pepper to taste
- 2 teaspoons dried marjoram
- 3 pounds venison, cut into 1/4 thick strips
- 2 teaspoons ground dried rosemary
- 1 (12 ounce) package pita breads, warmed

DIRECTIONS

1. Whisk together the olive oil, cumin, garlic, marjoram, rosemary, oregano, red wine vinegar, salt, and pepper in a large glass or ceramic bowl. Add the venison strips, and toss to evenly coat. Cover the bowl with plastic wrap, and marinate in the refrigerator at least 2 hours.
2. Heat a large skillet over medium-high heat. Cook the venison strips, a half pound at a time, until the venison has browned on the outside and is no longer pink on the inside, about 8 minutes. Pile the meat onto warmed pitas to serve.

LUNCH BOX HOT HOT DOGS
Servings: 1 | Prep: 5m | Cooks: 10m | Total: 25m

NUTRITION FACTS

Calories: 384 | Carbohydrates: 25.6g | Fat: 24.4g | Protein: 15g | Cholesterol: 48mg

INGREDIENTS

- 1 all-beef hot dog
- 1 packet prepared yellow mustard
- 1 hot dog bun
- 2 tablespoons shredded Cheddar cheese
- 1 packet ketchup

DIRECTIONS

1. Prepare your child's lunch box by packing the hot dog bun, ketchup, mustard and Cheddar cheese.
2. Preheat your child's insulated beverage container by filling with boiling water. Let stand for 15 to 20 minutes. I put the kettle on when I get up and let it heat while the kids get ready for school. Right before they leave, dump out that water and replace with more boiling water. The preheating keeps it hot for a longer time. Place a hot dog into the water and close the lid.
3. When your child is ready for lunch, they can take the hot hot dog out of the container and place it on the bun. Top with ketchup, mustard and cheese to make a hot lunch from home.

PERFECT BREAKFAST
Servings: 1 | Prep: 10m | Cooks: 5m | Total: 15m

NUTRITION FACTS

Calories: 501 | Carbohydrates: 25.9g | Fat: 36.1g | Protein: 21.5g | Cholesterol: 402mg

INGREDIENTS

- 2 teaspoons butter
- Dijon mustard
- 2 eggs
- 1/2 avocado - peeled, pitted, and sliced

- 1 slice sourdough bread, toasted
- 2 tablespoons grated Parmesan cheese, or more to taste

DIRECTIONS

1. Melt 2 teaspoons butter in a skillet over medium heat; add the eggs. Allow the egg whites to cook until mostly firm before breaking the yolks; continue cooking until eggs are completely cooked and no longer runny, 2 to 3 minutes.
2. Spread one side of toasted sourdough bread slice with Dijon mustard.
3. Arrange avocado slice onto the mustard.
4. Top avocado with cooked eggs.
5. Sprinkle Parmesan cheese over eggs.

JEFF'S SLOPPY JOES
Servings: 8 | Prep: 10m | Cooks: 10m | Total: 20m

NUTRITION FACTS

Calories: 235 | Carbohydrates: 8.9g | Fat: 15.4g | Protein: 14.9g | Cholesterol: 46mg

INGREDIENTS

- 2 tablespoons olive oil
- 1/2 pound Italian sausage
- 1 cup chopped onion
- 1 (12 fluid ounce) can or bottle chili sauce
- 2 cloves garlic, minced
- 2 tablespoons red wine vinegar
- 1/2 cup chopped green bell pepper
- 1 tablespoon Worcestershire sauce
- 1 stalk celery, chopped
- 2 teaspoons brown sugar
- 1/2 teaspoon dried oregano
- salt and pepper to taste
- 1 pound ground beef

DIRECTIONS

1. Heat the oil in a large skillet over medium heat. Add the onion, garlic, green bell pepper, celery and oregano. Saute for 5 minutes, or until onion is tender. Transfer this mixture to a plate and reserve for later.
2. In the same skillet over medium high heat, combine the ground beef and sausage and saute for 10 minutes, or until well browned. Add reserved onion mixture, chili sauce, vinegar, Worcestershire sauce and brown sugar and mix well. Season with salt and pepper to taste.

SIMPLE TUNA MELTS

Servings: 4 | Prep: 5m | Cooks: 10m | Total: 15m

NUTRITION FACTS

Calories: 224 | Carbohydrates: 15.4g | Fat: 10.2g | Protein: 17.5g | Cholesterol: 39mg

INGREDIENTS

- 1 (5 ounce) can tuna, drained
- 12 slices pickled jalapeno
- 1/2 small onion, minced
- 2 English muffins, split
- pepper to taste
- 4 slices Cheddar cheese

DIRECTIONS

1. Preheat oven to 350 degrees F (175 degrees C).
2. In a small bowl, combine tuna, minced onion, and black pepper. Divide mixture onto 4 halves of English Muffins. Arrange 3 slices jalapenos on each muffin half. Top each with a slice of Cheddar cheese. Place on baking sheet.
3. Bake in oven for 10 minutes, or until cheese begins to bubble.

EASY STEAK SANDWICH

Servings: 1 | Prep: 10m | Cooks: 15m | Total: 25m

NUTRITION FACTS

Calories: 1196 | Carbohydrates: 95.8g | Fat: 57.7g | Protein: 74.3g | Cholesterol: 222mg

INGREDIENTS

- 2 tablespoons butter
- 3 tablespoons chopped pickled hot peppers
- 1/4 medium onion, sliced
- 1 teaspoon hot pepper sauce
- 4 large fresh mushrooms, sliced
- 2 slices sharp Cheddar cheese
- 1/4 green bell pepper, sliced into long strips
- salt and pepper to taste
- 1 (1/2 pound) well-marbled beef steak of any type, sliced as thinly as possible
- 1/3 French baguette, cut in half lengthwise

DIRECTIONS

1. Melt 1 tablespoon of butter in a large skillet over medium heat. Add the onion; cook and stir until tender. Push onion to the side of the pan, and add the mushrooms. Cook and stir until softened, then add the bell pepper and cook just until tender, about 3 minutes. Remove from the pan with a slotted spoon, and set aside.
2. Add the remaining butter to the skillet. No need to clean the pan, just let it heat up a little bit. Place the steak in the skillet along with the pickled peppers. Season with salt and pepper. The steak cooks really fast, just a couple of minutes. Once the steak is mostly browned, return the onion and pepper to the pan. Cook until heated through.
3. Turn off the heat, and place the slices of cheese over the top of the pile so they can melt. Scoop the whole pile into the awaiting bread, making sure to pour some of the juices onto that wonderful sandwich.

SLOW COOKER BARBECUE GOOSE SANDWICH
Servings: 3 | Prep: 5m | Cooks: 6h | Total: 6h5m

NUTRITION FACTS

Calories: 190 | Carbohydrates: 4.4g | Fat: 15.2g | Protein: 9g | Cholesterol: 51mg

INGREDIENTS

- 2 tablespoons butter
- 1 goose breast
- 1 clove garlic, minced
- 1 1/2 tablespoons Worcestershire sauce
- 1 small yellow onion, sliced
- 2 cups chicken broth

DIRECTIONS

1. Melt butter in a large saucepan over medium heat. Add garlic and onion and saute for 5 minutes. Add goose breast and brown on both sides for about 5 minutes, or until browned.
2. Place goose breast in slow cooker and add Worcestershire sauce. Add chicken broth to cover (approximately 2 cups) and cook on High setting for 6 to 8 hours, or until meat falls off bone. Shred with a fork and mix with your favorite barbecue sauce.

SLOW COOKER BARBEQUED PORK FOR SANDWICHES
Servings: 12 | Prep: 10m | Cooks: 7h | Total: 7h10m

NUTRITION FACTS

Calories: 224 | Carbohydrates: 22.3g | Fat: 9.2g | Protein: 10.6g | Cholesterol: 37mg

INGREDIENTS

- 2 1/2 pounds boneless pork roast
- 3 cups beef broth
- salt and ground black pepper to taste
- 1 cup water
- 2 cups strong brewed coffee
- 1 small onion, diced
- 2 tablespoons Worcestershire sauce
- 1 pinch crushed red pepper flakes
- 2 tablespoons bourbon whiskey
- 2 (12 ounce) bottles barbeque sauce
- 10 cloves garlic

DIRECTIONS

1. Season the roast with salt and pepper. Place the seasoned roast, coffee, Worcestershire sauce, bourbon whiskey, garlic, beef broth, water, onion, and red pepper flakes in a slow cooker set to LOW. Cook 3 to 4 hours. Scoop garlic cloves out of the cooker and mash with a fork; return the mashed garlic to the slow cooker. Cook another 3 to 4 hours.
2. Transfer roast to a large cutting board, and discard liquid. Shred the roast into strands using two forks, and return meat to the slow cooker. Stir in the barbeque sauce, and continue cooking on LOW for 1 to 3 hours.

BANH MI

Servings: 2 | Prep: 30m | Cooks: 20m | Total: 50m

NUTRITION FACTS

Calories: 657.2 | Carbohydrates: 85.2g | Fat: 0g | Protein: 24g | Cholesterol: 42.8mg

INGREDIENTS

- 1/2 cup rice vinegar
- 1 pinch ground black pepper to taste
- 1/4 cup water
- 1 (12 inch) French baguette
- 1/4 cup white sugar
- 4 tablespoons mayonnaise
- 1/4 cup carrot, cut into 1/16-inch-thick matchsticks
- 1/4 cup thinly sliced cucumber
- 1/4 cup white (daikon) radish, cut into 1/16-inch-thick matchsticks
- 1 tablespoon fresh cilantro leaves

- 1/4 cup thinly sliced white onion
- 1 small jalapeno pepper - seeded and cut into 1/16-inch-thick matchsticks
- 1 skinless, boneless chicken breast half
- 1 wedge lime
- 1 pinch garlic salt to taste

DIRECTIONS

1. Place rice vinegar, water, and sugar into a saucepan over medium heat, bring to a boil, and stir until the sugar has dissolved, about 1 minute. Allow the mixture to cool.
2. Pour the cooled vinegar mixture over the carrot, radish, and onion in a bowl, and allow to stand for at least 30 minutes. Drain off the excess vinegar mixture after the vegetables have marinated.
3. While the vegetables are marinating, preheat the oven's broiler, and set the oven rack about 6 inches from the heat source. Lightly oil a slotted broiler pan.
4. Sprinkle the chicken breast with garlic salt and pepper, and broil on slotted broiler pan, turning once, until the center of the chicken breast is no longer pink and the surface has browned, about 6 minutes per side. Remove the broiled chicken, and slice into bite-size pieces.
5. Slice the baguette in half the long way, and pull the center of the bread out of the baguette halves, leaving a cavity for the filling. Place the baguette halves under the broiler to lightly toast, 2 to 3 minutes.
6. To assemble the bahn mi sandwich, spread each half of the toasted baguette with mayonnaise, and fill the cavity of the bottom half of the bread with broiled chicken, cucumber slices, pickled carrot, onion, and radish, cilantro leaves, and jalapeno pepper. Squeeze a wedge of lime over the filling, and top with the other half of the baguette.

ZESTY PULLED PORK SANDWICHES
Servings: 4 | Prep: 10m | Cooks: 4h30m | Total: 4h40m

NUTRITION FACTS

Calories: 504 | Carbohydrates: 78.6g | Fat: 9g | Protein: 25.7g | Cholesterol: 53mg

INGREDIENTS

- 1 1/2 cups barbeque sauce, or more as desired
- 1 teaspoon ground black pepper
- 1/2 cup chopped white onion
- 1/2 teaspoon chili powder
- 1/4 cup ketchup
- 1 pound boneless pork loin, quartered
- 1/4 cup brown sugar
- 4 onion rolls, halved
- 1 teaspoon salt

DIRECTIONS

1. Stir barbeque sauce, onion, ketchup, brown sugar, salt, black pepper, and chili powder in slow cooker; add pork loin and coat with sauce. Cover and cook on High until pork is very tender, about 4 1/2 hours. Shred pork with 2 forks. Keep warm on Low until ready to serve. Serve on onion rolls.

PEANUT BUTTER, MAYONNAISE, AND LETTUCE SANDWICH

Servings: 1 | Prep: 5m | Cooks: 0m | Total: 5m

NUTRITION FACTS

Calories: 428 | Carbohydrates: 33g | Fat: 29g | Protein: 12.4g | Cholesterol: 5mg

INGREDIENTS

- 2 slices bread
- 2 tablespoons peanut butter
- 1 tablespoon mayonnaise
- 2 lettuce leaves

DIRECTIONS

1. Spread one slice of bread with mayonnaise. Spread the other slice with peanut butter. Place lettuce leaves on top of the peanut butter, then top with the mayonnaise-side of the other piece of bread to make a sandwich

DALLAS-STYLE SLOPPY JOES

Servings: 5 | Prep: 20m | Cooks: 25m | Total: 45m

NUTRITION FACTS

Calories: 530 | Carbohydrates: 59.4g | Fat: 19.5g | Protein: 29.6g | Cholesterol: 85mg

INGREDIENTS

- 1 1/2 pounds lean ground beef
- 3 tablespoons Worcestershire sauce
- 1 yellow onion, chopped
- 3 tablespoons brown sugar
- 1 red bell pepper, chopped
- 3 tablespoons yellow mustard
- sea salt and ground black pepper to taste

- 3 tablespoons hickory flavored barbecue sauce
- 1 1/2 cups ketchup
- 2 tablespoons grated Parmesan cheese
- 3 tablespoons apple cider vinegar
- 5 large hamburger buns, toasted

DIRECTIONS

1. Cook the ground beef in a large skillet over medium heat until completely browned, 5 to 7 minutes. Add the onion and bell pepper, season with sea salt and black pepper, and cook until vegetables soften, about 7 minutes.
2. Stir in the ketchup, vinegar, Worcestershire sauce, brown sugar, mustard, and barbeque sauce. Reduce heat to low and simmer the mixture until thickened, about 10 minutes. Add Parmesan cheese and serve on toasted hamburger buns.

SUPER BLT

Servings: 4 | Prep: 10m | Cooks: 10m | Total: 20m

NUTRITION FACTS

Calories: 306 | Carbohydrates: 28.5g | Fat: 15.9g | Protein: 12.3g | Cholesterol: 36mg

INGREDIENTS

- 8 slices bacon
- 1/4 cup cream cheese
- 8 slices bread, toasted
- 4 lettuce leaves
- 1/4 cup guacamole
- 4 slices tomato

DIRECTIONS

1. Place the bacon in a large, deep skillet, and cook over medium-high heat, turning occasionally, until evenly browned, about 10 minutes. Drain the bacon slices on a paper towel-lined plate.
2. Spread the guacamole on 4 slices of toasted bread and the cream cheese on the remaining 4 slices. Arrange a lettuce leaf, tomato slice, and two pieces of bacon on top of 4 slices of bread and top with the remaining slices.

TUNA EGG SANDWICH

Servings: 2 | Prep: 5m | Cooks: 10m | Total: 15m

NUTRITION FACTS

Calories: 389 | Carbohydrates: 26.4g | Fat: 16g | Protein: 33.3g | Cholesterol: 340mg

INGREDIENTS

- 1 (5 ounce) can tuna, drained
- 1 tablespoon mayonnaise
- 3 hard-cooked eggs, peeled and chopped
- salt and pepper to taste
- 1 cup chopped celery
- 4 slices whole wheat bread

DIRECTIONS

1. In a medium bowl, stir together the tuna, eggs, celery and mayonnaise. Season with salt and pepper to taste. Place half of the mixture onto 1 slice of bread and the other half on another slice of bread. Top with remaining slices of bread. Serve.

MAD DOGS

Servings: 1 | Prep: 15m | Cooks: 15m | Total: 30m

NUTRITION FACTS

Calories: 478 | Carbohydrates: 1.5g | Fat: 44g | Protein: 19g | Cholesterol: 93mg

INGREDIENTS

- 1 hot dog
- 1 slice Cheddar cheese
- 1 slice bacon

DIRECTIONS

1. Preheat oven to 400 degrees F (200 degrees C).
2. Using a knife, make a slit along the entire length of the hot dog that's about 3/4 of the way through the hot dog. Break the cheese slice into 2 pieces and stuff each piece into the slit in the dog. Wrap the bacon slice around the hot dog in a spiral fashion, then secure all with a toothpick. Place on a cookie sheet or baking dish.
3. Bake at 400 degrees F (200 degrees C) for 11 to 15 minutes, or until bacon is crisp.

PBM SANDWICH

Servings: 1 | Prep: 4m | Cooks: 1m | Total: 5m

NUTRITION FACTS

Calories: 373 | Carbohydrates: 43.5g | Fat: 18.1g | Protein: 12.1g | Cholesterol: 0mg

INGREDIENTS

- 2 tablespoons peanut butter
- 2 slices bread
- 2 1/2 tablespoons marshmallow cream (such as Marshmallow Fluff)

DIRECTIONS

1. Spread the peanut butter onto one slice of bread. Spread the marshmallow creme onto the other slice. Place the bread topping-side-up onto a microwave-safe plate. Cook in the microwave on High for 30 seconds. Place the two halves together and serve.

TURKEY BACON AVOCADO SANDWICH
Servings: 1 | Prep: 15m | Cooks: 0m | Total: 15m

NUTRITION FACTS

Calories: 708 | Carbohydrates: 38.3g | Fat: 44.9g | Protein: 39.7g | Cholesterol: 93mg

INGREDIENTS

- 1 tablespoon reduced-fat mayonnaise (optional)
- 4 slices precooked bacon, microwaved according to package directions
- 2 slices bread, toasted
- 1/2 avocado - peeled, pitted, and thinly sliced
- 1 slice provolone cheese
- 1 slice ripe tomato
- 4 thin slices deli turkey breast
- 1 leaf lettuce

DIRECTIONS

1. Spread mayonnaise on one side of both slices of toasted bread. Top a bread slice with provolone cheese, turkey, bacon, avocado, tomato, and lettuce. Place the remaining bread slice on top, slice in half, and serve.

SISTER SCHUBERT'S SLOPPY JOES
Servings: 12 | Prep: 20m | Cooks: 45m | Total: 1h5m

NUTRITION FACTS

Calories: 483 | Carbohydrates: 58.3g | Fat: 14.2g | Protein: 31g | Cholesterol: 87mg

INGREDIENTS

- 2 (15 ounce) packages Sister Schubert's Dinner Yeast Rolls, prepared according to package directions
- 1/4 cup brown sugar
- 3 pounds lean ground sirloin
- 2 tablespoons vinegar
- 1 tablespoon vegetable oil
- 2 tablespoons Worcestershire sauce
- 3/4 cup chopped onion
- 2 tablespoons dry mustard
- 3/4 cup finely chopped green or red bell pepper
- 1 teaspoon salt or to taste
- 2 1/2 cups ketchup
- 1/2 teaspoon freshly ground black pepper
- 1/4 cup tomato paste
- 1 2/3 cups water

DIRECTIONS

1. Heat a deep skillet or Dutch oven over medium heat and add ground meat. Brown meat until it is cooked thoroughly. Carefully drain and discard fat. Transfer meat to a bowl.
2. To same pan, heat oil on medium heat; and add onions and peppers and cook 4 to 5 minutes, stirring frequently. When vegetables are tender, return meat to pan and add remaining ingredients. Stir frequently to cover meat with sauce. Reduce heat to low and cook for 20 to 30 minutes or until mixture thickens slightly.
3. Split Sister Schubert Dinner Yeast Rolls and spoon meat into rolls. Serve.

MIKE'S FAVORITE GRILLED CHEESE
Servings: 1 | Prep: 5m | Cooks: 5m | Total: 10m

NUTRITION FACTS

Calories: 549 | Carbohydrates: 26.2g | Fat: 42.4g | Protein: 16.6g | Cholesterol: 114mg

INGREDIENTS

- 2 slices bread
- 2 tablespoons butter, divided
- 2 slices processed American cheese

DIRECTIONS

1. Heat a small skillet to medium high heat. Spread a thin layer of butter on one side of both bread slices; place one slice bread, buttered-side-down, in hot skillet. Immediately place both cheese slices on bread and cover with second bread slice, butter-side-up. When first side is browned, turn over and brown other side. Remove from heat and let cool 2 to 3 minutes before serving.

POOR MAN'S SANDWICH

Servings: 1 | Prep: 5m | Cooks: 0m | Total: 5m

NUTRITION FACTS

Calories: 361 | Carbohydrates: 31.2g | Fat: 0g | Protein: 13.9g | Cholesterol: 3mg

INGREDIENTS

- 1 1/2 tablespoons creamy peanut butter
- 1 tablespoon thinly sliced onion
- 2 slices whole wheat bread
- 2 teaspoons mayonnaise
- 6 slices dill pickle

DIRECTIONS

1. Spread peanut butter onto one slice of the bread. Place pickle slices and onion slices onto the peanut butter. Spread mayonnaise onto the other slice of bread, and place on top of the other piece of bread.

Printed in Great Britain
by Amazon

46383805R00064